THE RESTORATION
OF
ARNOLD MIDDLETON

A Play

by

DAVID STOREY

SAMUEL FRENCH

LONDON
NEW YORK   SYDNEY   TORONTO   HOLLYWOOD

ISBN 0 573 01376 4

Printed in Great Britain by
Butler & Tanner Ltd, Frome and London

THE RESTORATION OF ARNOLD MIDDLETON

First produced at the Traverse Theatre, Edinburgh, on 22nd November 1966, with the following cast of characters:

(in order of their appearance)

MRS EDIE ELLIS	*June Watson*
JOAN MIDDLETON	*Marian Diamond*
ARNOLD MIDDLETON	*David Collings*
JEFFREY HANSON	*Paul Williamson*
SHEILA O'CONNOR	*Ann Holloway*
MAUREEN WILKINSON	*Rosemary McHale*

The play directed by GORDON MCDOUGALL
Setting by Denzil Walker
Lighting by Paul Miller

Subsequently produced at the Royal Court Theatre, London, on 4th July 1967, with the following cast:

MRS EDIE ELLIS	*Noel Dyson*
JOAN MIDDLETON	*Eileen Atkins*
ARNOLD MIDDLETON	*John Shepherd*
JEFFREY HANSON	*Tenniel Evans*
SHEILA O'CONNOR	*Gillian Hills*
MAUREEN WILKINSON	*Andree Evans*

The play directed by ROBERT KIDD
Setting by Bernard Culshaw
Lighting by Andy Phillips and Bill Dufton

SYNOPSIS OF SCENES

The action of the play passes in a room in the Middletons' house

ACT I

SCENE 1   Afternoon
SCENE 2   Evening

ACT II

SCENE 1   Late afternoon
SCENE 2   The same evening

ACT III

SCENE 1   The next morning
SCENE 2   Evening, a few days later

Time—the present

ACT I

SCENE I

SCENE—*A cosy, well-furnished, scrupulously clean living-room. Afternoon. The room is equipped with a dining-table and chairs, as well as a three-piece suite and sideboard. Arranged round the room, on the walls and furniture, are various objects, mounted and in an excellent state of preservation: a stuffed eagle, a sword, a ship, a model aeroplane, a model engine, etc., which may suggest the rudiments of a museum, but bereft of any specific human connotation. Over the sideboard hangs a Lee-Enfield rifle. The centre of the room is dominated by a full-sized suit of armour, standing in a pile of brown paper and string from which it has just emerged. A two-handed sword runs down from its hands.*

When the CURTAIN *rises,* JOAN *and* MRS ELLIS *are discovered regarding the suit of armour with a mixture of amazement and distaste.* JOAN *stands* R *of the figure. She is an attractive, good-humoured, tenacious-looking woman in her early thirties.* MRS ELLIS, *her mother, is* L *of the figure. She is a rather unconsciously sensual woman in her late fifties. Like her daughter, she is neatly and prettily dressed. Both women are also wearing pinafores.* JOAN'S *pinafore is full,* MRS ELLIS'S *petite and frilly and fastened around her waist.* JOAN *has a label in her hand.*

MRS ELLIS. Well . . .! They must have sent it here by mistake.

JOAN (*glancing at the label*) It's the right address.

MRS ELLIS. But it should have gone to the school, surely? That where he has all the others.

JOAN. The man said that he'd asked for it to be delivered here.

MRS ELLIS. Here? But why here? We've nowhere to keep it here. Whoever would want a thing like this in their house?

JOAN. Perhaps it's his idea of a joke. (*She looks round the room*) At this rate we shan't be here at all soon.

MRS ELLIS. He must mean it to go to the school, Joan. Eventually. That's where all the others are. And he's had it sent here so we can see it.

JOAN. Well, it's strange if he has, because it's the only one I've seen. Queen Elizabeth, George the Fifth and all the rest. I'm the only person who hasn't been allowed in. "Some other time. Some other time." While any schoolchild can go in and out as he pleases.

MRS ELLIS. I'm sure that's where this will end up. The history museum. Just you see.

JOAN. Clean the paper up, Mother, will you? I'll put his tea on.

(JOAN *goes into the kitchen* L. *She treats her mother strictly, as she would a servant*)

Mrs Ellis (*clearing up*) Well, it's a surprise, and no mistake.

Joan (*off*) Have you got all the string? I don't want bits left lying about.

Mrs Ellis (*looking up at the armour as she stoops*) Of course . . . It's as you say. His idea of a joke. (*She laughs uneasily and moves above the sofa* R)

(Joan *enters with a tea-tray*)

Joan (*moving to the table*) Or an insult. (*She sets the tray on the table*)

Mrs Ellis. Insult? It needs time to sink in. I can see now . . .

Joan (*taking a tablecloth from the sideboard*) Could you put it all in the kitchen? There's a piece of string. (*She sets the table for tea. As she passes the suit of armour one way, she changes her mind and goes the other, as though it were a person to be avoided*)

(Mrs Ellis, *her arms full of brown paper, stoops down, retrieves the last morsel of string, and carries her load into the kitchen*)

Mrs Ellis (*off*) Of course, if you were really stuck for somewhere to put it, you could keep it in the bedroom.

Joan. In the bedroom!

Mrs Ellis (*off*) No-one would see it, would they?

Joan. No-one?

Mrs Ellis. Not in the bedroom.

Joan. What about me?

(Mrs Ellis *enters and moves behind the armour*)

Mrs Ellis (*picking up string*) Well. I'm sure I don't want to quarrel about it.

Joan (*lightly*) Well, then, at least I'm glad of that.

Mrs Ellis. I do live here as well, Joan.

Joan (*disregarding*) Could you do the bread? (*She checks her watch with the clock*) He'll have forgotten altogether that we're going out tonight.

Mrs Ellis (*moving to the table and buttering bread*) You're so inconsiderate, Joan.

Joan (*moving* R *of the sofa and picking up string*) It would be different, wouldn't it, if he ever showed any interest in them. But he spreads them all over the place, then never looks at them again. Accidentally move one and he comes down on you as though it were the house you'd shifted.

Mrs Ellis. Why can't you let it rest? He doesn't give you anything else to grumble about. You can't complain about him. Not really.

Joan. He's never out of the damned house. He puts on his coat, goes out to school, and leaves them like this. They're like spies. He never lets you rest. Everywhere you look there's some part of him watching and waiting. Even in the bathroom . . .

Mrs Ellis. It's just you, Joan, that.

Joan. Two slices. That's enough. (*Moving* R *of the armour*) Well, it's not staying there.

Mrs Ellis. Where are you going to put it?

Joan (*taking hold of the armour and leaning it back*) Don't just stand there. In the cupboard!

Mrs Ellis. In the cupboard! Do you think we should?

(Joan *and* Mrs Ellis *take the armour to the cupboard* R)

Joan. It's obscene. Something like this in the house. It makes you feel terrible just to touch it. These houses weren't built for things like this. Mother, will you open the door?

(*They put the armour in the cupboard and* Joan *hands out a few brushes, mops and an umbrella which she gives to* Mrs Ellis *before shutting the cupboard doors on the armour*)

Put those in the kitchen, will you?

Mrs Ellis. Are you going to hide it from him?

Joan. It'll do for now. Why did he have to have it here? Aren't there enough people here already?

(Mrs Ellis *exits* L *with the umbrella, brooms and mops*)

(*Straightening the sofa*) There's his mother and father coming in two days' time. Can you imagine what they are going to think?

(Mrs Ellis *enters to between the armchairs*)

Mrs Ellis. They'll hardly complain, Joan.

Joan. Coming to somebody's house only to find out as you step through the door it's a museum. It's not a home, it's an institution.

Mrs Ellis. They've never seen *either* of you all these years. They're hardly in a position to judge anybody.

Joan. But that's just what they will do. They're just about total strangers, aren't they? Come to that, it's just as well they are.

Mrs Ellis. I don't know . . .

(Joan *turns restlessly about the room*, Mrs Ellis *watching her concernedly*)

If only you had something.

Joan (*beginning to rearrange the tea-table already scrupulously prepared by both of them*) Had something what?

Mrs Ellis. An interest.

Joan. Interest! I have an interest.

Mrs Ellis. You could go out to work, get a job. You're qualified to do any number of things.

Joan. This is my house.

Mrs Ellis. I know it's your house, Joan.

Joan. And it takes some looking after.

(Mrs Ellis *does not answer*)

I run this as I want it.

MRS ELLIS (*moving below the table*) All I'm saying is I could run the house while you do something else. (*She begins to rearrange the table*) And there would be so much more coming in.

JOAN (*moving above the sofa*) And your widow's pension.

MRS ELLIS. I don't just mean money. (*Moving above the table*) But all those opportunities for other interests as well.

JOAN. You think, then, we'd all be better off if we each had an interest?

MRS ELLIS. What's life for if you can't have an interest?

(JOAN *examines her mother shrewdly*)

JOAN. You know, Mother, you're too much like me.

MRS ELLIS. People can laugh at interests, but it's like religion. He who laughs . . .

JOAN (*shouting*) We've got an interest here already! *His!* It's scattered in every cranny of this building. You can't sit down without finding a stone "with an interesting mark" on it, or a bit of wood that fell off Noah's ark, or a rotten old nail that dropped out of somebody's rotten old chariot. And just look at that thing. Standing behind that cupboard door listening to every word I say. It's not fair. It's not fair.

MRS ELLIS. Joan, I do my work here.

(*They are silent for a moment*)

JOAN (*sitting in the armchair* C; *contemplatively*) Do you remember once when you bought him a little statue—a man's head and shoulders? God only knows where his body had got to. And he accidentally knocked it off the sideboard and broke it?

MRS ELLIS (*moving* R *of the table and above the sofa*) He was more concerned with my feelings than with the thing.

JOAN. He wanted to get rid of it.

MRS ELLIS. He did not.

JOAN. He wanted to get rid of it. It was the only thing that resembled a human being in the entire house.

MRS ELLIS. You've never understood him, Joan. You never have.

JOAN. And now he brings this thing. There's something strange about it. It's the first lifelike thing he's ever had here. He usually keeps them all at school. (*She rises and goes to the hall for her coat*)

MRS ELLIS. Joan. You don't understand my position here. (*Moving* L *of the sofa*) Where are you going?

JOAN (*in the hall*) Out. (*She puts her coat on over her pinafore*)

MRS ELLIS. If you're hoping to go to the cinema, you'll have to leave almost as soon as he comes in. He'll be back any time now.

JOAN (*moving to the mirror* L) I won't be long. He's not going to find me waiting here, that's all.

MRS ELLIS. Waiting here?

JOAN. Stuck here amongst his trophies. I'll go down to the corner, or something. (*She moves to the kitchen door*)

MRS ELLIS. It's ridiculous.

JOAN (*turning to her*) I'll go out the back way, then there's no chance of meeting.

MRS ELLIS. Joan. This is silly. (*Suddenly, looking at the cupboard*) You won't be long, will you, Joan?

JOAN. Don't mention *that* until I come in. (*She indicates the cupboard*) Do you understand?

MRS ELLIS. Yes. But . . .

JOAN. And for God's sake don't say I've just gone out. Say I've been gone an hour. All right?

(JOAN *leaves by the kitchen door*)

MRS ELLIS. You won't be long, love, will you?

(MRS ELLIS *picks up the string from the sofa, puts it in the sideboard drawer, glances at the cupboard again, then goes to the table, fingers and rearranges the various tea-things, then moves uncertainly about the room, avoiding the cupboard area completely. Finally she comes face to face with the mirror, glances at it, then becomes increasingly interested in her reflection. She begins to examine her face, its various expressions of hope and dismay, glee and uncertainty, unconsciously producing animal noises, purring and cooing. She becomes lost in herself; her body heaves for a sigh, then suddenly relaxes in a huge, vaguely grotesque smile. ARNIE, a well-built man in his thirties, appears in the hall doorway. He watches a while, expressionless, then comes quietly into the room until he is almost behind Mrs Ellis. Then he suddenly barks like a dog. MRS ELLIS gives a scream of fright*)

Oh, Arnie! Arnie!

ARNIE (*putting his coat and briefcase on the sofa*) Loved one!

MRS ELLIS (*recovering*) It's just what you'd expect from a school-master.

ARNIE. Master, Edie. (*Picking up the coat*) Master. Watch this, Edie.

(*Using his coat as a whip*, ARNIE *begins to beat the floor*. MRS ELLIS *watches this with interest and pleasure, yet as though she's seen it all before*)

Take that. And that. And that—you sniffling snot-gobbling little crat. And that. I'll teach you to take my stick of chalk. (*He growls and roars as he drives the imaginary child into the floor. He steps on the spot and spreads the remnants thoroughly over the carpet*) Now. How do you like that, Edie? I know how to take care of these little crats.

MRS ELLIS. I don't know. It's a wonder any of them stay alive.

ARNIE. Know? Edie! You know. (*He puts his coat on the sofa*) You know everything.

MRS ELLIS (*pleased*) What! Me!

ARNIE. You.

Mrs Ellis. More than a schoolteacher?

Arnie. Yes.

Mrs Ellis. Well—I don't know . . . (*She holds her cheek with pleasure*)

(Arnie *watches her, suddenly intent*)

Arnie. Look . . . (*His mood relaxes again*) Did you see his face? The way he looked when I hit him the first time. He thought I didn't mean it. He thought I'd *let him off* for taking my stick of chalk. Mind you—he'd every reason to think I wouldn't beat his lousy head in. These *dwarfs* think you're frightened of being reprimanded, of being handed over to the . . .

Mrs Ellis. And will you get the sack?

Arnie. No such fortune for me. (*He sits down on the sofa and begins to tug off his shoes. His mood changes again, and becomes reflective*) If I rape two, or perhaps it may have to be three, I might be asked if I'd mind being moved to another school. But chances of promotion like that are increasingly rare. (*He gets his last shoe off with a struggle*) Rape apart, it's all a question of dead men's shoes, Edie.

Mrs Ellis (*moving* c; *concernedly*) I wish you wouldn't use language like that, Arnie.

Arnie (*holding up his shoes*) Ill will; that's the cargo these shoes carry. Along, that is, with my own personal misfortunes. (*He searches round, sees Mrs Ellis's feet, and, on hands and knees, crawls across to them as though they were shoes he was hunting*) Why—why, these are full of hopes.

Mrs Ellis. Oh, now . . .

Arnie (*kneeling in front of Mrs Ellis*) Can't you feel them; growing beneath your feet? Why, Edie, your shoes are full of hope. It's sprouting through your toes . . .

Mrs Ellis. All I feel is how glad I am I didn't know what teachers were like when our Joan went to school.

Arnie (*sitting on the sofa*) Where is *she*, by the way? Not gone off on my bike, her dress tucked into her bloomers.

Mrs Ellis. Really, Arnie! She's just gone out. I mean, *merely* gone out.

Arnie. Merely gone out?

Mrs Ellis. She's only gone out. That's what I mean.

Arnie. Only gone out. Not merely gone out.

Mrs Ellis. She's—out.

Arnie. I see.

Mrs Ellis. Your tea's on the table.

(Mrs Ellis *exits to the kitchen*)

Arnie (*rising*) We're supposed to be going to the cinema. Let me see—(*consulting his wristwatch*)—half an hour ago.

Mrs Ellis (*off*) She'll only be a few minutes . . .

Arnie (*knowingly and quickly searching the room*) It all seems very carefully timed. What's going on?

Mrs Ellis (*off*) She's so restless. She can't sit down two minutes these days without getting up again because there's something not satisfactory. I don't know . . . it's just everything.

(Arnie *turns at this and goes to the table. He sits down* R *of it and begins to put some jam on the bread*)

How's your play going at school?

(Arnie *plays with the bread abstractedly.* Mrs Ellis *enters from the kitchen door with a teapot and a poached egg*)

You. (*Moving below the table to* R *of Arnie*) Can't you hear me when I talk to you?
Arnie. What's that, chump-chops?
Mrs Ellis. None of your cheek. (*She moves round Arnie to above the table*) Haven't you been rehearsing this afternoon?

(Arnie *breaks his mood to give a dramatic recitation*)

Arnie. Said Robin Hood to Friar Tuck,
    "How are you my fat fellow?"
    "I'm very well," said the cheerful monk,
    "But I'm sorry you're looking yellow."

    "Is that a jest or would you dare
    To challenge your captain staunch?"
    "Nay," said the Friar, "don't threaten me,
    Or I'll kill you with my paunch."

Mrs Ellis (*giggles*) Is that it? (*She pours two cups of tea*)
Arnie. A generous portion of it, Edie. On the whole, I think it will appear neither conspicuous nor insignificant on the contemporary theatrical scene.
Mrs Ellis. Is it going very well?
Arnie. A minor alarm this morning when the Lionheart tripped over his scabbard. He'll appear on stage with a bandage round his leg—a wound sustained while fighting the Turks outside Damascus.
Mrs Ellis. They're only boys. (*She moves* R *of the table and sits below it*) What are you calling the play?
Arnie. I don't know. (*Thoughtfully*) "Hands up, Sheriff, your Money or your Wife."
Mrs Ellis. Oh, now.
Arnie. "The Good King Richard and the Bad King John." Probably "Robin Hood and his Merry Men", Edie.
Mrs Ellis. Oh, that's nice. (*Watching him eating his tea*) And is it adapted from William Shakespeare, then?
Arnie. No. Jeffrey Hanson. He's the head of the English Department. He's coming round tomorrow evening to discuss the less serious aspects of the play. So that'll be tea for two, Edie.
Mrs Ellis. Oh, I'll be out late tomorrow, getting things in.

(*Silence*) Are you looking forward to them coming? Are you listening?

ARNIE. Yes.

MRS ELLIS. What are they like?

ARNIE. Who?

MRS ELLIS. You know. Silly.

ARNIE. Oh. (*He dismisses it*)

MRS ELLIS. Of course, I only met them that once at the wedding. Ten years. (*She broods*) It's not often you meet decent people nowadays. (*Suddenly*) You complain that they never come to see you. Yet you've never been to see them.

ARNIE. No.

MRS ELLIS. Did you have a happy childhood, Arnie?

ARNIE. Did you?

MRS ELLIS (*laughing*) No: I'm asking you. I bet you were a model child.

ARNIE (*pleasantly*) I was. Facsimiles of me could be seen all over the place at one time, Edie.

(MRS ELLIS *becomes preoccupied with her thoughts, getting up and wandering round the room distractedly*)

MRS ELLIS. You know, Arnie . . . (*She moves above the sofa to* C)

(ARNIE *takes out a pipe and looks round*)

Joan. She's been in such a funny mood today. (*She moves* LC)

ARNIE. Yes.

MRS ELLIS. You've stopped listening, haven't you?

ARNIE. I have not.

MRS ELLIS. She's been suggesting, you know—that I wasn't much use to anyone.

ARNIE. You know, Edie, I've told you before. I'm not stepping in between your women's fights.

MRS ELLIS (*moving above the table*) Do you want another cup?

ARNIE. Thanks.

(MRS ELLIS *pours a cup.* ARNIE *fusses with his pipe*)

It would be nice to have a proper job and a decent home, wouldn't it?

MRS ELLIS. Arnie! You have a decent home. And it could be even better if you'd let me.

ARNIE. Better?

MRS ELLIS. Cleaner and neater.

ARNIE. Cleaner than this? (*He stirs up his tea with milk and sugar*)

(MRS ELLIS *watches him acutely, the teapot still in her hand*)

MRS ELLIS. In a way.

ARNIE. In a way! Why can't we ever hold a decent conversation in this house. I teach in a madhouse all day, then come home to another at night.

Mrs Ellis (*outraged*) Arnie!

Arnie. It's not right. You and Joan . . . If you would only say what you meant. Just once.

Mrs Ellis. You don't begrudge me staying here, do you?

Arnie. No.

Mrs Ellis. I could go away. I'm not so old . . .

Arnie. Edie. (*Rising and moving* L *to between the chairs*) What are you talking about?

Mrs Ellis. Fancy . . . Do you remember that little statue I bought you once as a present. That was accidentally broken.

Arnie. What?

Mrs Ellis (*moving* C) Joan said—this afternoon—that you broke is deliberately. Because you didn't like it. And you hadn't the heart to tell me.

Arnie. Now, look, I don't have to stand here and listen to all this, Edie. You're a woman in your own right: you must stick up for yourself.

Mrs Ellis (*clearly upset*) I don't want to cause any bother. I don't. But Joan's always making me feel I haven't got anything at all . . . nothing.

(Arnie *watches her. Then he moves to her and takes her shoulders*)

Arnie. I didn't break it on purpose, Edie. And it wasn't a statue. It was a piece of pottery made to look like stone. I appreciated you giving it to me. All right?

(Mrs Ellis *looks into his eyes, then nods*)

So there's no need to start an argument, is there?

Mrs Ellis. No.

(*The front door bangs, and* Arnie *releases her.* Joan *enters the hall and removes her coat*)

Arnie. Quick. Hide under the table and tickle her knees.

Mrs Ellis (*laughing*) Get on with you, you devil! (*She moves to the table and starts to clear it*)

(Arnie *takes a comic from his pocket and sits on the sofa.* Joan *enters the room*)

Arnie (*reading like a child*) G . . . g . . . g . . . gooood . . . ness g . . . g . . . g . . . gra . . . gra . . . gracious! Ssss . . . ssss . . . ssssaid th . . . th . . . th . . . the F . . . ffff . . . Fff . . . Fairy Qu . . . Qu . . . Qu . . . Queen.

Joan. That girl's followed you home from school again. I suppose you realize.

Arnie (*putting down the comic*) What? (*He rises and moves to the window up* C)

Joan. O'Connor. Isn't that her name?

Arnie (*looking out*) I don't know what I'd do without her. Always

that faithful twenty-five yards behind. Like a progressive following
the revolution.

(MRS ELLIS *joins Arnie to look out, too*)

JOAN. She moved smartly across the road when I came in. And
no wonder.

MRS ELLIS. What does she hope to get out of it?

ARNIE (*moving to the sofa and picking up the comic*) Some people do
things, Edie, not for what they can get but for what they can give
. . . (*He moves to the door*)

JOAN. Oh, very nice. For two damn pins I'd go out there and give
her something she *wouldn't* be grateful for! And I thought we were
going out tonight?

ARNIE. I'm ready when you are. I'll just finish this instalment,
then I'll be right with you.

JOAN. Is that a child's magazine?

ARNIE. It's all right. I didn't buy it. I stole it from a desk.

(ARNIE *exits to the hall and off* R. *His feet are heard going upstairs, then
a door slams.* JOAN *moves to the window*)

JOAN. Has he seen that?

MRS ELLIS. No.

JOAN. Are you sure?

MRS ELLIS. I'm positive.

JOAN. What have you been crying about?

MRS ELLIS. I haven't been crying. (*She finishes clearing the table*)

JOAN. It doesn't look like that.

MRS ELLIS (*moving below the table*) We were talking about his
parents, if you must know.

JOAN (*moving L of the table*) What about his parents?

MRS ELLIS. Nothing you would understand.

(JOAN *watches her intently*)

JOAN. I don't like this. I don't.

MRS ELLIS. What?

JOAN. This! This! (*She grabs and tugs at her mother's pinafore*)

MRS ELLIS. What?

(JOAN *does not answer*)

What's the matter with . . .

JOAN (*moving down L*) It's all wrong!

(*For a moment neither of them can speak*)

MRS ELLIS. I'll take mine off, then.

JOAN. Take *yours* off?

(MRS ELLIS *takes her apron off slowly: she lays the petite-looking thing
absent-mindedly on Arnie's raincoat on the sofa*)

Not there! Not there! (*She snatches it up and throws it on the floor*)

MRS ELLIS. Joannie . . .

JOAN. I don't like this. I don't.

MRS ELLIS. What is it, pet?

JOAN. Don't *pet* me.

MRS ELLIS. Joan . . .

JOAN (*moving below the sofa to* R) You weren't talking about his parents. You were talking about *me*. (*She moves above the cupboard*)

MRS ELLIS. Do you think we've nothing better . . .

JOAN. Don't say *we*! You were talking about me. You were talking to him about me. Did you tell him—did you say anything about that? (*She gestures at the cupboard*)

MRS ELLIS. No.

(ARNIE'S *feet are heard stamping down the stairs.* MRS ELLIS *moves to the radiogram.* ARNIE *enters, smoking a pipe, moves to the sofa, and sits, putting on his shoes*)

ARNIE. Well, ready?

JOAN. I have a surprise for you first.

ARNIE (*genially*) Yes.

(MRS ELLIS *moves between the armchairs*)

JOAN. Are you ready?

ARNIE (*rising*) Yes—just a minute. (*He sits* L *of the table, facing the cupboard*) Right.

JOAN. All right?

ARNIE. Yes.

(JOAN *swings open the cupboard doors*)

JOAN. There.

ARNIE (*smoking on*) Oh, that's where it is.

JOAN. How do you mean, that's where it is?

ARNIE. I couldn't imagine where you'd hidden it. It wasn't upstairs; I've just looked.

JOAN (*crying out at Mrs Ellis*) You told him! You liar!

ARNIE. As a matter of fact, I asked the man to ring up the school and let me know when he delivered it.

JOAN. You *sneak*!

ARNIE. I'm not sneaking. I've been waiting for it to come.

JOAN. You rotten, bloody sneak. I've been walking around out there . . .

ARNIE. Walking round?

JOAN. What's it doing here?

ARNIE. Walking *round*?

JOAN. What's it doing *here*?

ARNIE (*rising*) Walking round? (*He puts his pipe in his mouth*)

JOAN What's it doing here?

ARNIE (*moving to the cupboard and taking the armour out*) It looks to

me as though it's standing in a cupboard. (*To the armour*) Aren't
you coming in, old man?

JOAN. I mean *here*! Here! At this house. You usually have all this
junk thrown into your mausoleum at school.

ARNIE. But I didn't buy this with school funds.

JOAN. What?

(ARNIE *moves the armour* C *and stands* R *of it*)

ARNIE. It's mine. I bought it myself.

JOAN. Yours? (*She moves* L *of the armour; after a pause*) What sort
of talk is this, Arnold?

ARNIE. I've always wanted one.

JOAN. When did you buy it?

ARNIE. What?

JOAN. When did you buy it?

ARNIE. A few days ago.

JOAN. Why? What for? Don't you think we've enough with this
already?

ARNIE. You're very aggressive, Joan. Has it assaulted you or
something behind my back?

JOAN. It's going back where it came from.

ARNIE. It even smokes a pipe. (*He puts his pipe in the armour's visor
and moves down* R) I told you it was respectable. I don't know. It
might easily entertain political ambitions. (*He moves* C *and begins
detaching the sword*)

JOAN. I've tolerated everything else, Arnie, but not this.

(ARNIE *takes no notice, busy detaching the sword*)

Can't you see? The place isn't built for a thing like this.

(ARNIE *leaps* LC *with a shout and swings the sword at* MRS ELLIS,
who escapes with a scream)

MRS ELLIS. Arnie! (*She runs* L)

(ARNIE *snorts at Mrs Ellis*)

JOAN. Where do you think you're going to keep it for one thing?
In the garden?

MRS ELLIS. Oh. We can't keep it there. (*She jumps*) Joan! Every-
body would see it.

JOAN. And I'm not having it in the kitchen, peering over my
shoulder. And not in the bathroom, the bedroom, the living-room or
the hall.

(ARNIE *stalks Mrs Ellis*)

MRS ELLIS. No, Arnie! No!

ARNIE (*holding the blade to Mrs Ellis*) D'you think it's blood? (*He
moves* L *of Joan*)

JOAN. It's not staying here, Arnie. It's ugly. That's enough!

ARNIE (*moving* R *of the armour*) Well. Are we ready? (*He fits the sword back into place*)

JOAN. Ready?

ARNIE. To go out.

JOAN. Are we going out now? And leave this?

ARNIE. What do you want me to do? (*He moves down* R) Hug it and give it a kiss? It won't run away. Well, Edie . . . how about you, then?

MRS ELLIS. Going out? I don't mind going out. Why, it's ages . . .

JOAN. It's all right. (*She goes to the hall*) Tomorrow, first thing: that's going. (*She puts on her coat*)

ARNIE (*picking up his coat from the sofa*) Aren't you going to take your apron off?

JOAN. What? (*She returns to* L *of the sofa*)

ARNIE. Your how d'you do.

(JOAN *sees she still has on her pinafore, takes it off and puts it on the sofa*)

Don't you want to come, Edie?

MRS ELLIS. Well . . .

(JOAN, *watching her mother, pulls on her coat*)

JOAN. She'll be quite all right at home.

MRS ELLIS. I wouldn't have minded going out. I don't really fancy being left alone with this, Arnie.

ARNIE. Get your coat, Granny, and away we go!

MRS ELLIS. Aye, now . . . (*She goes to the hall for her coat*)

ARNIE (*putting his arm round Joan*) It's not half as bad as it seems.

JOAN. It's too much, Arnie, that's all. (*But she is appeased by his coaxing gestures*) Stop playing around . . .

ARNIE. O sing us a song, you hearty woman,
      Of all your dark crimes and your fears;
      And we'll swallow our pride and lie down by your side,
      And digest all your grief in our tears.

JOAN. Do you hear . . .

(MRS ELLIS *returns with her coat*)

ARNIE. Ah, now, a gorgeous old lady of twenty-one . . .

MRS ELLIS (*moving between the armchairs*) Inches round the neck. I know.

ARNIE. Oh, now, Edie. You enlargen yourself . . . (*He goes to help her with her coat*)

MRS ELLIS. Oh, I know. Don't worry. I wasn't born yesterday.

ARNIE. If you insist.

MRS ELLIS. There you are, you see. And I ought to have done my face.

ARNIE. Only a disservice, my dear.

MRS ELLIS. Goodness. What's got into him?

(ARNIE *takes Mrs Ellis's hand*)

ARNIE (*moving up* C) Pray take advantage of my goodwill:
    Let us share it between the two;
    Take all you can and in return
    I'll do the same for you.

JOAN. Come on, we better be going out before he breaks into song.

ARNIE. A moment. (*He sidles with exaggerated caution to the window, carefully lifts the net curtain, and looks out*) The coast's clear. (*To Joan*) Your glance spoke as eloquently as your thoughts, my dear. Her loyalty knew no bounds—and now you've presented it with several.

(JOAN *and* MRS ELLIS *move to the door*)

JOAN. At least we can go out now, without being molested.

ARNIE. You always could. It's me who is the loser.

(ARNIE *puts his arms round Joan and Mrs Ellis and moves with them into the hall*)

    Gay Robin Hood to town did ride
    With maidens fair on either side:
    The evil Sheriff and the bad King John
    Ne'er recognized the gentlemon.

(JOAN *waits patiently by the front door*)

(*Hesitating*) Yes.

ARNIE *sweeps Joan and Mrs Ellis out of the house. A moment later, however, he dashes back in, knocks his pipe out on the armour, boxes it briefly, pats it, then hurries out, shutting the room door. His voice is heard crying with pleasure, then a door crashes to, and it is silent. The room slowly darkens, as*

the LIGHTS *fade to Blackout.*

SCENE 2

SCENE—*The same. Evening.*

The stage is in darkness, and the room is empty. After a moment the front door bursts open and there is giggling and laughter. MRS ELLIS *and* ARNIE *enter and move down* L.

ARNIE (*switching on the lights*) We should—we should—we should . . .

MRS ELLIS. But we didn't. (*She breaks into outrageous laughter*)

(JOAN *enters*)

JOAN. We'd have been home a damn sight sooner if we had. Weee! (*She throws her shoes into the air and runs below the table*)

ARNIE (*moving LC; instructionally*) If we had, we wouldn't have had to stand all the way back. (*He belches*)

JOAN. I'll be sick if I drink any more. (*She sits on the sofa*)

MRS ELLIS. It was your idea.

ARNIE (*moving L of the table*) She doesn't have ideas, Mother. Only prejudices.

(JOAN *barks angrily like a dog at Arnie, snarling, then growling*)

MRS ELLIS. Whatever anybody says, I enjoyed myself. I enjoyed myself. (*Telling herself*) How about you, Joan?

(ARNIE *takes off his jacket*)

JOAN. All the time—all the time—asking each other if we've had a good time? All the way back—(*mimicking*)—"Have you had a good time, Arnie? Have you had a good time, Edie?"

ARNIE (*replacing the chair L of the table and putting his jacket on the back of it*) Well, have you had a good time, Edie? (*He moves R of Mrs Ellis*)

JOAN. What did you call me?

(ARNIE *takes Mrs Ellis by the shoulders and looks into her face*)

You called me Edie!

(ARNIE *turns from Mrs Ellis, one hand still holding her shoulder, and he begins to recite with a boy's mechanical, tutored gestures to an imaginary audience*)

ARNIE. I have lived a long time, Mother,
  And seen strange sights beyond the seas,
  But never a one have I seen, Mother,
  To match the dimples in your knees

(MRS ELLIS *bursts out laughing*)

JOAN (*calling out*) You called me Edie, you swab!

ARNIE. There are women who shout and women who moan,
  And women who titter down the phone,
  But the only women that I ever see
  Are the ones that need hanging from the nearest tree.

JOAN (*rising*) You're disgusting!

ARNIE. My wife Joan has a heart of stone,
  And eyes as black as *charcoal*,
  She wouldn't have looked bad (*Moving R of the armour*)
  If she hadn't have had
  A mouth the shape of her . . . (*He whistles*)

JOAN (*advancing on Arnie*) I'll kill you!

ARNIE (*leaping behind the armour*) If you touch me I'll set him on to you.

JOAN. And tomorrow that thing's going first thing.

ARNIE. He'll tear you to pieces!

(*For a moment they stand poised, silent*)

MRS ELLIS. I think you both better get to bed.

(JOAN *moves away* R)

ARNIE. Did you hear . . . (*He steps cautiously from behind the armour, reassures himself from Joan's look that he is safe*) Did you hear as we passed them in the street what those—*children* called me? Children—I might add—whom I teach and instruct in my own classroom.

(JOAN *moves to the table and takes off her coat*)

MRS ELLIS. It's nothing I'd care to repeat.

(JOAN *takes a bottle from her pocket and drinks*)

ARNIE. And it's nothing, I can assure you, Mother, that I've taught them. Those words are not in the curriculum. I even thought once that they liked me.

JOAN. You shouldn't go round getting plastered where they can see you.

(ARNIE *takes Mrs Ellis's hand suddenly*)

ARNIE. Here—here, darling.

(ARNIE *leads Mrs Ellis to the chair down* L *and sits her in it*)

> There are things in your life
> Not even your wife
> Would think could pass through your brain.
> But give me a light
> And I'll show you a sight
> That would turn even Satan insane.

(MRS ELLIS *laughs, shocked, and rises*)

MRS ELLIS. I think I'll be getting to bed . . .

JOAN (*moving* R *of the armour*) Oh, no, Mother.

MRS ELLIS. What?

JOAN. You're not going to bed till you've helped me shift this.

(MRS ELLIS *moves* L *of the armour*)

ARNIE. Where to?

(JOAN *and* MRS ELLIS *move the armour back to the cupboard*)

JOAN. I'm not going to bed, I'm not. I'd never rest. Not with this wandering loose in the house.

ARNIE. What's it going to get up and do?

JOAN. It's going back in its kennel. And tomorrow—

ARNIE }
JOAN } (*together*) { —morning it's going out first thing.

(ARNIE, *still bleary with drink, watches ironically, arms folded, as* JOAN *and* MRS ELLIS *struggle to the cupboard with the armour*)

ARNIE. Rub-adub-dub, three nuts in a tub,
Who do you think they can be? (*He moves to the radiogram* L *and switches it on*)

JOAN (*struggling*) I've told you. Tomorrow morning—

ARNIE }
JOAN } (*together*) { —it's going out first thing.
You don't seem to believe me. But it is. The minute you've gone to school.

(*Dance music starts as the women haul the armour slowly to the cupboard.* ARNIE *begins to dance, taking a bottle from his jacket pocket and drinking*)

And I don't want to see it again. Do you hear? (*She hiccups*)

(ARNIE *dances on, oblivious to them.* MRS ELLIS *moves down* R *and watches, amused.* JOAN *fastens the cupboard door, then moves to the table for her bottle*)

MRS ELLIS. That's a sight for sore eyes. He can hardly put two feet together.

(MRS ELLIS *laughs, then claps.* ARNIE *looks up at her with sultry affection, eyes half closed*)

ARNIE (*dancing across* C *to Mrs Ellis*) Oh, I don't know—all that there and so forth. Hup-dee. Hup-dee.

JOAN (*hiccups*) Do you hear? (*She moves* LC)

(ARNIE *takes* MRS ELLIS's *hand and they dance loosely together,* MRS ELLIS *laughing still*)

ARNIE (*swaying his hips*) That's it, Edie. That's it. Swill it all around. Give it a good shake.

(JOAN *seems about to use her bottle on both the radio and Arnie, then some instinctive coquettishness overcomes her, and, bottle dangling, she puts her arm round Arnie.* ARNIE *spouts his own bottle to his lips*)

JOAN. Move over, babe. (*She bumps her mother*) Let's have a dance, honey.

(*The three of them, holding together, dance slowly and lugubriously*)

ARNIE. Sing us a song, Joannie.

JOAN. I can't sing . . . (*She hiccups*) I can't sing. (*She makes several near-noises approximating to the music*)

ARNIE. Oh, lovely, beautiful. (*He belches*)

(MRS ELLIS *dances away* L *on her own; a slow waltz, not ungraceful.*

She holds her skirt and dances with a slow nostalgia, moving between the chairs and back)

Oh, lovely, Edie. Lovely.

(MRS ELLIS *dances on to down* R. JOAN *and* ARNIE *stop to watch her, intrigued*)

JOAN. Go on, Mother. Let 'em have it. (*She hiccups*)
MRS ELLIS (*dancing*) Do you like it?
ARNIE. Go on, Edie. Don't stop. She's good. She's good. Oh, she's good. Just look at her little old legs going!
MRS ELLIS. What's the matter with my legs?
JOAN. You should see yourself, darling.
ARNIE. Take no notice of her, Edie. They're all right. You can take my word for it.
MRS ELLIS (*stopping* R, *and looking down at her legs*) I've got good legs—I always have had, since I was a young woman.
JOAN. Mother!
MRS ELLIS. What's the matter? (*She lowers her skirt*)
JOAN (*moving* L *of Mrs Ellis; with sudden bravado*) Those (*She hiccups*) are legs, if you want them! (*She lifts her skirt discreetly and poses her legs*) There's no comparison. Lift your skirt up. Lift. Come on. (*She pulls at her mother's skirt*)

(ARNIE *moves* L *to the radiogram*)

Lift. Pull it up. Just look. Arnie. What do you say? (*She hiccups*) *Hold* it up, mother. (*She turns round, for the first time aware of* ARNIE's *lack of attention*) Go on. What do you think? (*Pause*) Arnie, for God's sake.

(ARNIE *switches off the radiogram and blearily turns round*)

ARNIE. What . . .
JOAN. What do you say?

(MRS ELLIS *turns to him, holding her skirt, like a child paddling, her mood a vague stupor between elation and tiredness*)

ARNIE. What . . .
JOAN (*with one hand still guardedly holding her mother's skirt, the other her own*) Look, damn you!

(ARNIE, *overcome with weariness, moves to* L *of Joan*)

Tell her, for God's sake.
ARNIE. Tell her . . . ?
JOAN. What you think.
ARNIE. You want me to, Edie?
MRS ELLIS. I don't mind, love. (*She giggles*) It's getting draughty here.

(MRS ELLIS *and* JOAN *move down* R)

Joan. Look, look. We're walking. How's it look?

(Arnie *sits in the chair down* l, *drunkenly and tired. He watches, frowning, and belches*)

Arnie. Like a camel.

(Arnie *finishes off the bottle, toasting the cupboard doors*)

Joan. Just look at her, then. Mother, you walk up and down. And keep your skirts up.

(Mrs Ellis *and* Joan *walk to Arnie with their skirts up.* Joan *suddenly becomes aware of Arnie's diversion*)

You're not watching! (*She hiccups*) For God's sake. We're walking! Here! Give me that! (*She snatches the bottle from him*) All gone. Pig. (*She throws the bottle down, and suddenly snatches his hair*) Now—choose!

(Arnie *sinks down in the chair, calling out.* Mrs Ellis *moves above the* c *chair*)

Who's got the best legs! (*She hiccups*)
Arnie. Help! Let go! You're hurting! Yarooo!
Joan (*dragging Arnie from his chair to* c) I'm going to hurt you. Open your great mouth and tell her.
Arnie. Edie! Tell her to let go. She's drunk. She doesn't know. *OW!*
Mrs Ellis. Why don't do as she says, Arnie?
Arnie. *OW!*

(Joan's *grip tightens.* Arnie *falls to his knees.* Mrs Ellis *goes to the sideboard and picks up a pair of scissors*)

(*His humour still apparent, though he is more helpless than he had realized*) For God's sake let go, Joan. I'm an historian.
Joan. Choose. (*She hiccups*)
Arnie. If you don't let go, I'll maim you.
Joan. You try, then.
Mrs Ellis (*moving down* r *laughing, and holding her skirt as if paddling*) If you hold him still, I can cut his hair!
Joan. Go on, then, Mam . . .
Mrs Ellis. I'll cut it all off, Arnie!
Arnie. Get off!
Joan. Go on, Mam. Give him a cut. (*She hiccups*)

(Joan *pulls at his hair and* Arnie *gives a real cry of pain, and can only bend more ineffectually to the floor.* Joan *holds up the hair while, one-handed—her other holding up her skirt—*Mrs Ellis *cuts it off*)

Mrs Ellis. There! There! He looks younger already!
Joan. And another. Go on, Mam.
Arnie. Let go. Or I'll kill you. Both of you.
Joan. Go on, then. You stupid devil.

Mrs Ellis. Choose, Arnie. Then she'll let you go.

Joan. Choose!

Arnie. Edie! She's got the best legs. All the way.

Joan (*letting go of Arnie*) What? (*She hiccups*)

Arnie. Edie's! Edie's all the way.

Joan. You prefer *her* to me!

Arnie. Completely. (*He remains still kneeling, clutching his head, still humoured, considering how best to take his revenge*)

Joan (*with a hiccup*) You don't love *me*!

Arnie. No!

Joan. You've never loved me!

Arnie. Never!

Joan. You just wanted *that* (*She hiccups*) and then it was all over.

Arnie. Absolutely.

Joan. You don't love me.

Mrs Ellis (*chastened*) Let's get to bed. For goodness' sake. We're not in our senses. Come on. Let's get up.

Joan (*moving down* R) Yes. Yes! I know—I know . . .

Mrs Ellis. Joan . . .

(Joan *hiccups*)

Arnie (*rising*) Make way! Make way! Move back!

Joan. You've never loved me.

Arnie. Oh! Oh! Oh!

Joan. I know what's going on. Don't worry.

Arnie (*moving between the sofa and the chair* C) Why? Why? Why? All the time! Nothing but this, baby!

Mrs Ellis (*moving down* L) Take no notice. None of you. It doesn't mean anything. It's nothing.

Joan (*to Mrs Ellis*) Well, what are you doing here, then? (*She hiccups*) Come on. Come on. You be honest just this once.

Mrs Ellis. Joannie! Joannie!

Joan. History or no bloody history. Don't think I haven't noticed. (*She hiccups*) And that thing! All the time. Stuck in there listening to every word. (*She gestures at the cupboard*)

Arnie (*moving to the door*) I'm going up . . .

Joan. Arnie. Tell her. Tell her to go.

(Arnie *pauses on his way to the door*)

Tell her to go. (*She hiccups*)

Arnie (*after a pause*) If your Bob doesn't pay our Bob that bob that your Bob owes our Bob, our Bob will give your Bob a bob on the nose.

Joan. Arnie! Tell her! Tell her!

Arnie.   Tiger, tiger, burning bright,
            In the forests of the night:
            If you see a five-pound note
            Then take my tip and cut your throat.

JOAN. Tell her to go!
MRS ELLIS. No, Arnie!

ARNIE.   The man in the moon has a chocolate spoon,
           And eyeballs made of custard;
           His big fat head is a loaf of bread,
           And his whiskers are peppered with mustard.

JOAN. Arnie!

(ARNIE *pauses again, bows to them with a flourish*)

ARNIE. Ladies. Ladies. Ladies.

(ARNIE *exits, slamming the door*)

JOAN. Arnie!
MRS ELLIS. Arnie!

CURTAIN

ACT II

Scene 1

Scene—*The same. Late afternoon.*

When the Curtain *rises,* Jeff Hanson *is discovered slumped in the chair* c.
*He is about forty, a middle-aged man with certain perhaps obsessive desires
to retain his youth. He is dressed in a sports coat and flannels, and wears his
bowler hat: he also wears a very long scarf and yellow gloves—the eternal
student—but the scarf and gloves are at present on the chair* lc. *He retains,
besides the bowler on his head, a stout walking-stick which he uses to amplify
and reinforce his conversation. The suit of armour is standing behind him.*
Arnie *is sitting* r *of the table, smoking his pipe.* Joan *is out of sight in
the hall, polishing.*

Hanson (*with raised voice*) My dear Joan, I wouldn't believe a
word of it.

Joan (*off*) It was absolutely nothing at all.

Hanson. Absolutely.

Joan (*off*) We were drunk.

Hanson. Of course.

Joan (*off*) We'd all had too much.

Hanson. Naturally.

(Joan *appears in the door*)

Joan (*crossing down* r *to polish the coffee-table*) So whatever he's told
you . . .

Hanson. My dear china, he's told me nothing. All we've heard
are hints from you.

Joan (*watching Arnie suspiciously*) You never know . . .

Hanson. And if he had it would be of no account. (*Indicating
Arnie*) Our long friendship is based on the simple precaution that
I never believe a single word he says. I hate to indulge in scepticism
of any sort, but events have always justified my foresight.

Arnie. He's lying as dexterously himself . . .

Hanson. Arnold, I'm the last person to step between a man and
his mother-in-law, as well you know. Despite all your accounts of
domestic felicities I have always refrained from intruding. The only
reason I don't agitate my hands about my ears is the faint hope that
I may hear an explanation . . . (*He looks steadfastly at Arnie*)

Joan. Of what?

Hanson. A remarkable occurrence that took place at school this
morning, my dear. (*Suddenly looking up at Joan*) I'm astonished
you're not already acquainted with it.

Joan (*watching Arnie*) Well, I'm not.

ARNIE. It was nothing.

HANSON. Nothing!

ARNIE. A slight miscalculation.

(JOAN *moves to the sofa and leans over the* L *arm*)

HANSON. My *dear* Joan—hardly were we assembled in the hall—eight hundred *youthful* spirits about to make the most *hearty* obeisances to the one and only—when what should we glimpse through the door backing on to the stage but the most incredible apparition you can imagine! Beyond the Headmaster's stout and noble figure—its eyes raised, somewhat prematurely it now appears, towards the Heavens—could be discerned a man accompanied by a suit of armour, stealthily creeping by under the obvious delusion that our devotions concealed him from our view. At first our benevolent autocrat mistook the huge and hideous roar that greeted this astonishing sight for one of religious fervour, his eyes travelling quickly downwards in a mixture of horror and surprise. (*He pauses*) Standing there in all his furtive glory was Arnold, smiling shyly in the arms of his new-found friend, and making unmistakable gestures with his one free hand that we should ignore his presence as best we may. *God in heaven*, I said to myself, is this a manifestation—the not-unforeseen consequence of our rigorous vocation—or has Arnold, my dearest and closest friend, taken complete and utter leave of his senses?

ARNIE. She wanted to get rid of it. I had to protect it the only way I could. If I hadn't have taken it to school, she'd have thrown it away.

JOAN (*rising and moving to the radiogram*) They must have laughed themselves sick!

HANSON. Except for the Head, my dear. (*Rising and moving* L *of the table*) Assuming it to be a comment upon his own austere regime —perhaps even on the strenuous nature of his religious practices—he ordered its immediate seizure and removal from the premises. It spent the remainder of its day, I believe, in the coal cellar, until its owner could take it home. (*He looks expectantly at Arnie*) Well?

(ARNIE *puffs contentedly at his pipe*)

Aren't you going to tell us? (*He pauses*) Is it some cheap means, Arnold, of publicizing your subject at the expense of others on the curriculum? (*He pauses*) Perhaps an indication to us of the kind of company you actually prefer.

ARNIE. I've told you why I took it to school.

JOAN. You won't get anything out of him.

HANSON. What is this, Arnold? Are we no longer sufficient for you? Your dear wife, your friends, your devoted pupils . . . Or is it that you feel a sword is necessary to prompt us to a proper admiration of your extraordinary talents. Ungrateful may be the world, but, Arnold, surely not those who know you.

ARNIE. It won't be here much longer. You better take advantage of it while you can.

JOAN. Not here? (*She pauses*) Where's it going?

HANSON. Not—back to school?

ARNIE. No.

JOAN. Where, then?

ARNIE. As a matter of fact, it's a present.

JOAN. A present!

HANSON. A present. Not for . . . (*He gestures at himself*)

ARNIE. No.

HANSON. Nor . . . (*He gestures at Joan*)

ARNIE. For my parents.

JOAN. Your parents!

ARNIE (*rising and collecting up his books, briefcase, and papers*) That's the last I want to hear of it. (*He moves to the coffee-table*)

HANSON. But—of course, I'm not acquainted with the couple— and far be it from me to judge from preconceptions. But are they—I mean, is it something they've always wanted? Do they have a fondness for metallic men?

JOAN (*crossing down R to Arnie*) You've never said it was a present. You never said it was.

ARNIE (*putting his briefcase under the coffee-table*) I take it I'm entitled to a little privacy of intention.

JOAN. Privacy of *what*?

HANSON. You mean they collect suits of armour.

JOAN. You let me shout down the house. (*Catching hold of him*) Look—have you just invented this?

ARNIE. That's all I want to hear of it. I've told you. (*He sits on the coffee-table*) Now you know. It's a present.

JOAN. He's always inventing things when he thinks it suits him. Why . . .

ARNIE. It's over.

JOAN. My God!

HANSON (*moving to the radiogram*) All these alarums, then, were merely to conceal the natural benevolence of your heart. What stratagems men will go to to disguise their proper virtues!

(JOAN, *however, is watching Arnie with a mixture of disbelief and condemnation*)

JOAN. Do you expect me to believe that? What's the point of buying them that? Of all things.

(ARNIE *does not answer*)

Aren't you going to talk? (*She pauses*) All right. (*Crossing L*) Just do as you damn well please. And tell him to take his hat off in the house.

(JOAN *exits to the kitchen.* HANSON *takes off his hat and puts it on the chair down L. There is a clink of cups from the kitchen.* HANSON *moves down R*)

Hanson. Have at you, man!

(Hanson *thrusts at Arnie with his stick*)

Arnie (*rising*) Have at you!

(*They fight with much groaning and exertion,* Arnie *with his invisible sword,* Hanson *with his stick*)

Back! Back! Th . . . th . . . th . . . i . . . i . . . i . . . ssss . . . ssss This! i . . . i . . . i . . . ssss . . . is! g . . . g . . . g . . . gay! r . . . r . . . r . . . r . . . Robin h . . . h . . . h . . . h . . . Hood!

(Hanson *gives a great and ugly scream and dies writhingly in the chair* c. Arnie *collapses on the sofa*)

Hanson. Actually, could you lend me five pounds?
Arnie. I haven't a cent. It all went on this.

(Hanson *rises and moves* r *of the chair. He eyes the armour suspiciously*)

Hanson. Oh. (*He pauses*) Actually. Why did you buy it?
Arnie. As a present.
Hanson. For your parents?

(Arnie *nods*)

Mmmmm! (*He watches Arnie a moment*) The purpose of the loan was to entertain a lady. Temporarily, I'm without the wherewithal without.
Arnie. A lady?
Hanson. A Miss Wilkinson, to be precise.
Arnie. Not our Miss Wilkinson? From school?
Hanson. 'Fraid so. (*He talks a little in Joan's direction*) Naturally the school premises—where normally I make assignations of this nature—are the most propitious place for the dalliances I have in mind. (*Moving behind the table, looking at objects*) But of late old Thompson, despite rheumatism, a protopsic condition of the right eye, and an audibly leaking bucket, has acquired in stealth what he has so patently forfeited in spontaneity. The Park, though ample in resources, and open to all classes and creeds of men, is constant victim to the inclemency of the weather; the lady herself lives with elderly parents in a charming country cottage several miles from town; and my landlord resents frivolities of every nature. (*He moves down* r)
Arnie (*watching him cautiously*) She's a damn fit woman, I'm told, Jeffrey.
Hanson. You were correctly informed, what? While we clamber daily through the portals of our plight, she is nimbly leaping over bucks, vaulting-horses and horizontal bars as lightly as—a frog, say.
Arnie. I had always assumed her to be the soul of integrity, Jeffrey.
Hanson. I have a curriculum to straighten out with her.
Arnie. That would be nice.

HANSON. And her permission to examine the subject on an evening suitable to both.

ARNIE. I see.

(JOAN *enters* L *with a tea-tray and moves to the table*)

HANSON. So what's to do?

ARNIE (*perceiving Joan*) Entertain her here.

HANSON. In public?

ARNIE. A party. Or whatever festivities you feel she might approve.

HANSON. Tonight?

JOAN (*setting down the tray*) Is someone coming here tonight? (*She moves* L *of the sofa*)

ARNIE. It is a debt of honour I am endeavouring to pay with a frenzied bout of hospitality. Nothing more.

JOAN. What do you think all this is for?

ARNIE. All what?

JOAN. This! All this tidying up!

ARNIE. Any evidence of the pleasures we may have sustained will have long been removed by then.

(JOAN *stares at him in silence*)

JOAN. What *is* all this about, Arnie?

ARNIE (*to Hanson*) You might bring a few bottles with you, Jeffrey. No reason why your pleasures should not entertain our own particular miseries.

HANSON. Oh, but of course.

JOAN. There's your tea. (*Moving* L) If you want anything else, help yourselves.

(JOAN *exits to the kitchen.* HANSON *moves to the table to pour himself a cup of tea*)

ARNIE. (*loudly*) Talking of religious fervours. Miss O'Connor followed me home again today. The distance of twenty-five yards has increased slightly to thirty, perhaps even thirty-five. Idolatry, I fear, has given way to something verging on detachment.

HANSON. Sheila O'Connor—— (*He moves* L *of the sofa*)

ARNIE. The one.

HANSON. —is a girl——

JOAN (*off*) I've seen enough of that.

HANSON. —upon whom a mischievous deity has bestowed two attributes, the largeness of which in all humble deference—must be an embarrassment even to Himself. (*He salaams to the ceiling*)

(JOAN *enters* L *with a duster*)

JOAN (*crossing up* R *to dust the sideboard*) Is that how you talk about the children?

HANSON. A child in the eyes of the State, my dear, but a woman in the eyes of God.

ARNIE. She actually approached me at four o'clock, just as I was entering the staff room prior to retrieving my armour, and asked me to take her out. Tonight. (*He pauses*) Those are the first words that have passed between us.

HANSON. Oh, she's never asked me that. She never has.

JOAN. What arrangements did you come to?

ARNIE. I suggested we rendezvous at the picture palace at nine o'clock. "Nine o'clock sharp, mind!" I said sternly, if not officiously —reminding her as casually as I could that I had a position to maintain. As it so happened, she would have followed me into the staff room there and then if it hadn't been for the fact that old Manners was marking her arithmetic book along with several thousand others. "Oh, Sheila," he said, looking up obliquely from his tattered ledgers, "I've just got to yours, my dear. Would you like to stand by me while I glance through your problems?" Wherein she vanished in the twinkle of an eye.

(JOAN *moves above the sofa*)

HANSON. There are incentives to the profession the Minister never dreamed of.

JOAN. Yes. (*She moves* L *off the sofa*)

ARNIE. You're very contained, my little sparrow.

JOAN. I've to fly up there and finish the stairs if you don't mind, then fly back down and tidy here.

HANSON. A woman's work is never done!

JOAN. *What!*

HANSON. I—merely a tribute, my dear, to your—profession.

JOAN. God, I love you, honey. (*She blows Hanson a kiss*)

(JOAN *exits to the hall.* HANSON *rises, goes to the table and pours himself more tea*)

HANSON. Say, old man. Isn't your hair somewhat oddly arranged for an historian. Or, indeed, for a man?

ARNIE. What?

HANSON. You're not short of food, I take it. It appears someone has consumed two mouthfuls of your tonsure. (*He moves down* L)

ARNIE. It was a slight accident on the way to the kitchen.

(HANSON *holds up his walking-stick guardedly*)

HANSON. Ah.

ARNIE. Mind your own business, loppy-lugs.

HANSON. Snot-nose.

ARNIE. *Carpet-breath.*

HANSON. That's revolting!

(ARNIE *rises and goes to the table to pour tea*)

By such inadvertent gestures cancer is induced.
Secrets go bad and affect the very flesh.

ARNIE. Cabbage knuckles.

HANSON (*with his stick*) Have at you, Gay Robin!

ARNIE (*without gesture*) Have at you, Big John.

(*There is a pause.* HANSON *taps the armour reflectively. Then he glances at Arnie*)

HANSON (*crossing down* L) You think, then, it's conceivable I'm mistaken about Miss Wilkinson. One grave disadvantage is that she's physically so very fit. It would be imprudent continually to have recourse to this stout staff while she merely relies upon the dexterity of her limbs. But my daily exercises are entirely cerebral, whereas hers, day in, day out, are designed exclusively to extend the already phenomenal resilience of her physique.

ARNIE (*moving to the sofa with his tea and sitting*) It could be an advantage, no doubt, in one way. And then again, in another . . .

HANSON (*moving between the sofa and the chair* C) But you do not think it strange—(*He glances round*)—that women are gradually acquiring a physical superiority to men? Do you think . . . (*He goes to the door, listens, then returns to put his arm round the armour*) Do you think there's some sort of organization behind it?

ARNIE. A conspiracy . . .

HANSON (*moving between the sofa and the chair*) Which we are very foolish to ignore. (*He glances quickly behind him*) I mean, one hears so much of judo and professional equality these days.

ARNIE. Does the King know?

HANSON. The King? My dear Arnold, the very sources are corrupt. (*He sits* L *of Arnie on the sofa. Thoughtfully*) I mean, it can't have failed to have reached your attention that we—that is men *and* women alike—emerge at some point of our lives from the body of a woman. But has it also occurred to you that whereas we are always under this obligation to them, they are never under a reciprocal obligation to us? They, as it were, *divulge* us: whereas we—we are simply *exposed*. This is an extraordinary advantage bestowed on one sex at the expense of the other. (*Confidentially, as a spy*) Have you noticed that women live longer than men? (*He pauses*) They do not fight wars, only occasionally do they murder their fellows, and they seldom, unfortunately, commit rape. Relate this to our original observation that it is *they* who breed *us*, then things like politics and finance, even philosophy and art, become like playthings bestowed on us by women merely to amuse and divert our unbreeding functions!

ARNIE. What time are you meeting her?

HANSON. What? (*He glances at his watch*) Yes, I shall have to go. (*He rises and moves to the chair* L *for his scarf, hat and gloves*) It is one thing to sit there and smile at present danger. It's quite another to sit there until you are *gobbled* up.

(JOAN *enters and moves to Arnie*)

ARNIE (*quickly*) You have caught Jeffrey in the very act of leaving. (*He rises and crosses to between the sofa and the chair* C)

HANSON. Ah, I did not hear you dismount, madam. I must be about my business before it is about me. (*He suddenly turns round on Arnie with his stick*) On guard!

ARNIE. To be sure.

(HANSON *salutes with his stick.* ARNIE *puts his arm round Joan's shoulder.* HANSON *glances at them for a moment, then moves to Joan*)

HANSON. I shall take my leave quickly. Imagine I am killed in the street the moment I have stepped beyond the door, and allow that poignancy to inform your farewells. (*He takes Joan's hand and kisses it, salaams to Arnie, then moves to the armour and taps it lightly with his stick*) That, Arnold. That. I'm not altogether sure of. Well . . . (*He regards the armour thoughtfully for a moment, then moves briskly to the door*) Remember, no fisticuffs when I introduce Miss Wilkinson to this abode. And may all our cavortings be as discreet and as anonymous as alcohol allows.

(HANSON *bows ceremoniously and exists backwards, closing the door. A moment later the outer door shuts.* ARNIE *releases Joan, moves above the sofa and sits* R *of the table.* JOAN *watches him for a moment*)

JOAN (*lenient*) You needn't be afraid.
ARNIE. Afraid?
JOAN. Of showing in private the affection you display in public. (*She pauses*) I could have told him.
ARNIE. You could?
JOAN. I heard your "discussion" from the stairs. I could have told him how you came to lose your hair.
ARNIE. An embarrassment to both of us, I would have thought.
JOAN. Doesn't *he* ever grow sick of it?
ARNIE. Of what?
JOAN (*after a pause*) You despise him really. (*She moves to the table and picks up the tray*)
ARNIE. I do not.

(JOAN *watches him for a moment, then exits to the kitchen. A moment later she re-enters without the tray*)

JOAN (*moving* C) Has something sunk through all those layers at last?
ARNIE (*after a pause*) Has what sunk through which layers?
JOAN. Disgust.
ARNIE. You're being boring.
JOAN. Isn't it that underneath . . .
ARNIE (*calling out*) You're being boring! I've never known anyone make such commonplace observations in so revelationary a tone!

(*They are both silent for a moment*)

JOAN (*quietly*) Do you have any feeling left for me at all?

ARNIE. Are you trying to be frivolous?

JOAN (*after a pause*) You make me feel I don't exist. You hide away. You don't look. You show nothing but a parody of yourself. You deride even your own weakness. Isn't that self-contempt?

ARNIE. You're sickening.

JOAN. Am I . . .

ARNIE. You're sickening. Your allegories are sickening, woman.

JOAN (*crying out and gesturing at the room*) And what's this, then, but sickening! What's this?

(ARNIE *makes no response.* JOAN *watches him*)

(*More quietly*) If you'd just break up this—pretence!

ARNIE. What? What? What? What?

JOAN. Anything so long as you don't have to step up here. (*She gestures at herself*)

ARNIE. You think that's an eminence worthy of ascent.

JOAN. You did once. (*There is a pause*) Why do you stay with me, Arnie?

(ARNIE *watches her intently*)

Go on.

ARNIE. Go knot your nose.

JOAN. Tell me. Why do you stay here?

ARNIE. Run up a flag.

JOAN. Try and answer me.

ARNIE. Leave me alone.

JOAN (*slowly*) Why do you stay with me, Arnie?

(ARNIE *glances round at the doors*)

Well off you go, then.

(*There is a silence*)

ARNIE. I can detect a piece of dust. Wait a minute, yes. It's under the near left-hand leg of the dressing-table in your mother's bed-room: a quick outflanking manoeuvre and it will be within your grasp.

(*There is another moment of silence*)

JOAN. You must make yourself so *sick*.

ARNIE. Ladybird, Ladybird, fly away home!
    Your house is on fire and your children have gone.

(*Another moment of silence.* JOAN *waits patiently.* ARNIE *suddenly shouts with burlesque affectation, slamming the table*)

Will somebody get me out of here!
Help! Help! . . . HELP!

(JOAN *watches for a moment*)

Joan. It's not a game, is it?

Arnie. Leave me alone.

Joan. No. You run away instead.

Arnie. All right. (*He does not move. After a pause*) Assume I've run away.

Joan. You insulting little *snot*!

(Arnie *closes his eyes*)

(*Moving to* l *of Arnie*) Come on. Get down on your knees and cry. Do something to attract some *pity*. Come on. Get down. Cry! Come on. Cry, *baby*, cry!

(Arnie *turns his head away*)

Nobody's going to love you unless you show us *something*.

Arnie. Go away.

Joan. Let's have some rage. Isn't there anything in this world, Arnold, that you'd like to put right?

Arnie. Go away.

Joan. Come on, baby. Isn't there anything that offends you? Isn't there some tiny little wrong that can rouse your indignation?

Arnie. Get out.

Joan. Come on. *Make me sickening!*

Arnie. Hop it!

(Joan *moves nearer him; studies his face more closely*)

Joan. Just look. For God's sake, Arnie.

(*They are both silent for a moment*)

What are you frightened of?

(Arnie *makes no response*)

(*Quietly*) All right. All right.

(Joan *watches him, waiting for a response, then exits quietly to the kitchen.* Arnie *sits remotely at the table. After a few moments* Joan *re-enters. She watches him for a moment, sitting exactly as she left him, then moves above the chairs to* c)

As a start, Arnie—I suggest we get rid of all these. (*She indicates the objects*)

Arnie. Yes.

Joan. You agree, then.

(*There is a pause, then* Arnie *looks up*)

Arnie. Certainly.

Joan. Yes (*She seems about to start*)

Arnie. Not yet.

Joan. Isn't this the best time?

Arnie (*after a pause*) No.

JOAN. All right. When?

ARNIE. Tomorrow.

JOAN. After *they've* been.

ARNIE. Er—yes.

JOAN. You promise that?

ARNIE. Yes.

JOAN (*indicating the armour*) And this?

    (ARNIE *regards it in silence*)

ARNIE. That's going in any case.

JOAN. As a present.

    (ARNIE *makes no response*)

And if they won't have it?

ARNIE. What?

JOAN. I can't imagine they will. (*She pauses*) If that's what you really intend to do with it.

    (*Pause*)

ARNIE. They'll have it because I'm giving it to them.

JOAN. Oh.

ARNIE. I like it.

JOAN. Yes.

ARNIE. And I'd like them to have it.

JOAN. Suppose they don't.

    (*Pause*)

ARNIE. This is not a battle. I've acquiesced to what you want. You don't understand it, Joan. Do you?

JOAN. No, I don't.

ARNIE. They'll be pleased with it because I am. And the other way round.

    (JOAN *watches him*)

It's not a battle, you know. Some people are actually like that.

JOAN. Yes.

ARNIE. All right?

JOAN. I'll believe it when I see it.

ARNIE. I doubt it.

JOAN. Well then, while we're clearing everything away, there's one other thing. It's time my mother left and went and lived on her own.

ARNIE. What?

JOAN. In this case you'll just have to accept *my* word if you don't believe it.

ARNIE. She's harmless.

JOAN. It's time she went for all our sakes. (*She moves upstage* C) You'll be better off for it. I will. And so will she.

ARNIE. I don't want her to go. It'd break her bloody heart.

JOAN. I'm sorry. But she'll have to.

(*The outside door bangs*)

That's her now.

ARNIE (*rising*) Well, don't say anything to her. Not yet.

JOAN. It's my decision.

ARNIE. I've told you. Don't. (*He waits, almost threatening*) You understand?

(JOAN *makes no response. There are sounds outside the door, and* ARNIE's *mood changes abruptly as* MRS ELLIS *appears. She is smartly dressed, a fur round her shoulders, and she carries a full shopping-basket which she puts on the table.* ARNIE *greets her with a dashing gesture*)

(*Crossing Joan to Mrs Ellis*)

Here comes a spy to parry at our scheme: I shall retire, and make it—all a dream.

(JOAN *moves between the sofa and chair* C)

MRS ELLIS (*pleased*) Oh . . .

(ARNIE *exits to the hall with a flourish*)

(*Moving* L *of Joan*) What's got into him?

(JOAN *does not answer*)

It's a lovely evening out. A beautiful sunset.

(*There is a pause. The two women confront each other,* MRS ELLIS *with some perplexity*)

What's the matter?

JOAN. Let me help you off with your coat, Mother.

MRS ELLIS. What?

JOAN. Your coat.

Surprised, MRS ELLIS *submits, as the* LIGHTS *fade to a Blackout*

SCENE 2

SCENE—*The same. The same evening.*

When the LIGHTS *come up,* ARNIE, *in shirtsleeves and tieless, is lying on the couch with his head to* R. *The suit of armour has gone. There are sounds of* JOAN *working in the kitchen.*

JOAN (*off*) Aren't you going to get changed?

(ARNIE *makes no response, his eyes closed, apparently asleep.* JOAN *enters and moves to the mirror up* L. *She has dressed herself attractively and her hair is tied in a ribbon*)

Aren't you going to get shaved?

ARNIE (*his eyes still closed*) I thought you wanted no-one here. The place kept tidy and clean.

JOAN. I've changed my mind. Aren't you going to get ready at all?

ARNIE. Oh? (*He opens his eyes and watches her a moment*) They might never get here.

JOAN (*moving below the table*) My mother's gone out for nothing, then.

ARNIE. She didn't have to go out.

JOAN. She didn't feel like meeting people this evening. That's all.

(*Pause*)

ARNIE. The sacrifice of one old woman.

JOAN. She can look after herself.

(ARNIE *rouses himself, sitting up*)

ARNIE. You can't turn people out like that, that's all. Not when they rely on you. You either do it at the beginning or not at all.

JOAN. I'm not arguing about it.

ARNIE. That's settled then.

(ARNIE, *sitting on the couch, slaps his thighs and looks around contentedly. Then he puts his hands together and blows between them, hooting like an owl*)

JOAN (*after a few moments*) You know . . .

(ARNIE *hoots*)

(*After a pause*) With my mother it's my decision whether she goes or not. She's *my* mother.

ARNIE. I've told you.

JOAN. But it's my decision, Arnie. I make it!

(*The door is crashed back on its hinges* HANSON *puts his head round*)

HANSON.   *Pray!* Hold thy hand, good Robin Hood,
          And your merry men each one,
          For you'll swear this is the finest maid
          That ever your eyes fell on.

JOAN. Don't you usually knock when you come in?

HANSON (*moving to Joan and taking her hand*)
          If thou will forsake, housewife, thy craft,
          And now to the greenwood with me. (*He kisses Joan's hand*)
          Thou shalt have loving all the year long,
          And forty gold crowns for thy fee.

ARNIE (*rising and moving down* R) All right. All right.

HANSON (*to Arnie*)
          And Robin leapt up full thirty good foot,
          'Twas thirty good foot and one,
          And he cleft the rude fellow with a blow of his fist—

(He moves to the door)

And his light went out like the sun.

(He goes out into the hall)

Go on, dear, straight ahead.

(SHEILA O'CONNOR enters. She is a precociously developed girl, though by no means loutish. Her shyness tends to disappear first when she sees Arnie, then the interior. She moves L of the chair C)

SHEILA. Hello, sir.

(MAUREEN WILKINSON enters, followed by HANSON. The school-mistress is dressed tastefully: a respectable and fairly attractive woman in her late twenties. HANSON stands L of Sheila, and MAUREEN L of Hanson)

ARNIE. Oh, hello, Sheila. Didn't expect to see you here.

HANSON. Odd thing. Passing the gate just as we came in. Thought: what a coincidence! Then: why one be damned when rest sanctified by celebration!

ARNIE. Yes. *(To Joan)* This is Sheila O'Connor, Joan. This is my wife, Sheila.

SHEILA. Hello, miss.

JOAN. Hello, Sheila.

ARNIE. Evening, Maureen. I don't think you know my wife. Joan —this is Maureen.

(JOAN crosses to Maureen)

MAUREEN. It's very nice meeting you, Joan.

(JOAN and MAUREEN shake hands)

JOAN. Let me take your coat. *(She does so)*

ARNIE *(to Hanson)* Well, let's sit down, and so forth.

(JOAN takes Maureen's coat into the hall)

HANSON. Look here, Arnold, would you mind awfully if Sheila and I betook ourselves to the hostelry to purchase an armful of drinks. Things came up. Distracted the intention . . .

ARNIE *(to Sheila)* So soon arrived, so soon departed.

HANSON *(taking Sheila to the hall)* You don't mind, do you, Sheila? I swear I heard you had been appointed milk monitor this term for the lower fifth.

SHEILA *(going into the hall)* It's not far, is it?

HANSON. Good girl! We shan't be long. Adios, caballeros.

ARNIE. Shall I . . . *(He moves above the sofa)*

HANSON. Oh, we'll manage, old man.

(HANSON and SHEILA exit. JOAN comes into the room and moves R to sit on the sofa)

JOAN. Does that irritate you?

MAUREEN. Oh, you get used to it.

JOAN. What is it, do you think?

MAUREEN (*sitting on the armchair* C) The school play this year is "Robin Hood and His Merry Men".

JOAN. No, I meant . . .

ARNIE (*almost vindictively*) You're being unnecessarily adventurous, aren't you, coming out with Jeffrey?

MAUREEN. He's asked me out so often it's less tedious to agree.

ARNIE (*moving* R *of Maureen*) Is that all.

MAUREEN. I'm sorry.

(JOAN *watches Arnie's almost vindictive manner with Maureen, curious and intrigued*)

There was nothing I could do about him bringing Sheila in. It's very foolish.

ARNIE. It'll give her a break from her usual sentry go. I never know whether she's keeping me in or keeping the others out.

JOAN. It's inviting trouble—walking through the streets with her like that, and going into pubs.

MAUREEN (*pleasantly*) Oh, he'll take a pleasure in it.

JOAN. After all, we're partly responsible for it.

ARNIE. Of those two, the only one who can be violated is Jeffrey.

MAUREEN. You're not responsible. That's absurd.

JOAN (*indicating Arnie*) Oh, he has ways of encouraging her. Don't worry.

ARNIE. She asked *me* out.

JOAN (*to Maureen*) Some days they say it's because they teach in a school; then on other days they say it's the world.

MAUREEN. I never knew you had a philosophy, Arnold. As well as a suit of armour. (*Stretching round*) Where is it, by the way?

ARNIE. Yes. (*He wanders uneasily about the room, moving above the table, then to* R *of it*)

JOAN (*to Maureen*) Are all your men staff alike?

MAUREEN. Oh, very nearly!

JOAN. Doesn't it wear you down?

MAUREEN (*laughing*) I shouldn't worry about it, Joan.

ARNIE. Watch this.

(ARNIE *does a handstand against the cupboard, balancing precariously. The women pause to watch*)

JOAN (*after a moment*) Would you like some tea, Maureen?

MAUREEN. Love some.

JOAN (*rising and crossing* L) I'll just put the kettle on. I was hoping to make some sandwiches as well. Won't be a minute.

(JOAN *goes into kitchen.* ARNIE *lowers himself from his handstand.* MAUREEN *looks round at the objects in the room for the first time*)

MAUREEN (*rising and moving above her chair*) Are all these yours?
ARNIE. Yes. (*He sits on the floor by the cupboard*)
MAUREEN. Don't you want me here?
ARNIE. You?
MAUREEN. Us.
ARNIE. It was *my* party. Joan has appropriated it.
MAUREEN (*laughs*) Yes.
ARNIE (*rising and moving* C *above the sofa*) Do you know what happened to the Early Christian martyrs the moment they stopped throwing them to the lions, and loved them instead?
MAUREEN (*moving* R *to the coffee-table*) They went off into the desert to live in caves haunted by demons.
ARNIE. What?

(MAUREEN *waits*)

I've told you before. (*He pauses*) Are you sure?
MAUREEN. Yes.
ARNIE. I see. (*He pauses*) Don't you think it's extraordinary?
MAUREEN. In what way?
ARNIE. In what way? (*He pauses*) I don't know really. It seemed extraordinary at the time . . .
MAUREEN (*after a pause*) Where is . . .

(JOAN *enters.* ARNIE *moves* L *of the table and picks up his jacket*)

JOAN. I'm making some sandwiches, then perhaps one or two people won't get so drunk.

(ARNIE *moves to the door* L)

Where are you going?
ARNIE. Out. (*He moves to the mirror*) See if Hanson needs any help.
JOAN. I should think he'd be able to manage well enough on his own. You won't be long?
ARNIE. No. (*He goes to the door*)
JOAN. Give us a kiss, Arnie.
ARNIE (*to Maureen*) You'll notice. Always the diminutive.

(MAUREEN *sits* R *on the sofa.* JOAN *waits.* ARNIE, *after a moment, comes back, takes her shoulder and kisses her on the cheek*)

JOAN. You won't be long, Arnold?
ARNIE. No.

(ARNIE *exits up* L. *There is a pause.* JOAN *tidies the cushion on the chair* LC)

JOAN. His parents are coming tomorrow. (*Moving* C) We haven't seen them for years. (*She sits in the chair* C)
MAUREEN. The best thing is to ride with it, isn't it? I still live with my parents; I know what a trouble they can be.

JOAN. When *we* got married and his mother came up to kiss me as we were leaving the church, she said, "Well, you'll look after my only son, won't you, Joan?" And he said quick as a flash, "Your only sin, Mother." And she smiled as sweetly as anything, he laughed out loud, and God! did I feel a fool! You can see just what a state I'm in. (*Rising*) Would you like to see round the house?

MAUREEN (*rising*) Yes, I'd love to.

(*They move to the hall*)

JOAN. I'll show you upstairs. You've seen nearly all there is to see down here. Considering how small they look from the outside it's surprising how large they are.

(JOAN *and* MAUREEN *exit to the stairs off* L)

MAUREEN (*off*) Do you intend staying on here, then?

JOAN (*off*) Oh, I suppose so. We've lived here since we got married. There's no point in moving into something smaller. This is the main bedroom—

(*Their voices grow fainter, then disappear. After a short interval there is the sound of the back door opening in the kitchen and, a moment later, the kitchen door is cautiously opened.* MRS ELLIS *enters. She's drunk. She puts a bottle on the table and stands aimlessly looking round, stifling her sobs with a handkerchief. Then she moves to the mirror and stares distractedly at herself, moaning. From above come the voices of* JOAN *and* MAUREEN *as they move about*)

—the bathroom there, and this is the spare room . . .

MAUREEN (*off*) Well, that's convenient. Goodness. Is that all Arnold's too?

JOAN (*off*) And this is my mother's room . . .

(MRS ELLIS *swings round, hurries to the kitchen door, then across to the door leading to the hall. Then, as* JOAN *and* MAUREEN *begin to descend the stairs, she remembers the bottle, hurriedly retrieves it and goes out by the hall door, leaving it open.* JOAN *and* MAUREEN *enter the room*)

MAUREEN (*moving* L *of the chair* C) His classroom's extraordinary. More like the court of King Arthur than a schoolroom. Have you seen his museum?

JOAN (*moving* R *of the chair* C) No.

MAUREEN. The children love it. What it has to do with history I've no idea. They seem to spend all their time building model castles, singing ballads and doing great big pictures of William the Conqueror. It's strange we've never met at school, isn't it? You've never been to any of the plays Arnold's produced, have you? They're very good.

JOAN. He prefers me to stay away.

MAUREEN. Whatever for?

Joan (*shrugs*) He prefers it, that's all. He's full of prejudices, you know, Maureen.

Maureen. Prejudices?

Joan (*moving* L) We'd better do the sandwiches, by the way, before they get back. The kettle should be boiling. You promise . . .

(Joan *and* Maureen *go into the kitchen. After a moment* Mrs Ellis *enter up* L *and stands hesitantly in the room, uncertain whether to go into the kitchen herself. She stifles a sob, staring at the door. Then, at the sound of a door opening and whispers from the hall, she glances wildly round and, with her bottle, departs unsteadily to the stairs. The sound of the women's laughter comes from the kitchen, and* Maureen's *shout of* "Joan!" Hanson *appears in the hall door, looks* L *and* R, *then signals behind him. He carries several bottles. Giggling,* Sheila *follows him in, a carrier bag with bottles in her arms.* Hanson *puts his finger to his lips and gestures at the kitchen.* Hanson *and* Sheila *cross* R)

Hanson (*moving to the coffee-table* R; *whispering*) Excellent. Very good, O'Connor. Next week, as a very special reward, you can be in charge of the ink *and* the chalk—and if you're extra good, I'll let you clean the blackboard. (*He puts the bottles on the table*)

Sheila (*putting her bottles on the table*) Oh, thank you, sir! (*She takes off her coat*)

Hanson. I think for that you deserve a red star. Or is it a green one.

(Hanson *pins an imaginary medal on Sheila's chest and then kisses her on either cheek.* Arnie *enters quietly up* L. Sheila *takes Hanson round the neck and kisses him more directly.* Hanson *looks up in mid-kiss and sees Arnie*)

There you are, dear fellow.

Arnie. Saw you down the street. Thought: bound to resent my intrusion. Kept my distance. Circumspect. All that.

Hanson. Absolutely, old boy. (*He takes Sheila's coat*)

Arnie. Not at all.

Joan (*off*) Arnie?

(Joan *enters from the kitchen with a tray of tea-things and sandwiches.* Maureen *follows with a teapot*)

There you are.

(Joan *and* Maureen *move* L *to the table and put down the tray and teapot*)

Maureen. Arrived back all together.

Hanson. Are we supposed to drink out of our hands?

Joan. You can help yourself in the kitchen.

Sheila (*moving* L) Can I find the glasses?

Hanson (*taking Sheila's coat into the hall*) You find them, love.

Anything that will hold liquid. You know what liquid is, don't you?
(*He moves* R)

SHEILA. Course I do, silly.

(HANSON *and* SHEILA *giggle.* SHEILA *exits down* L. ARNIE *moves the sofa and chair* C *lightly*)

JOAN. What are you doing?

ARNIE (*nodding his head at everyone, his face set in a pleased grin*) Just getting it all organized. Shipshape. Everyone on the best of terms. Pleasantries, cordialities, sparks within a fire. (*He rubs his hands energetically*)

JOAN (*to Arnie*) What's got *into* you.

(ARNIE *moves up* C)

MAUREEN (*to Hanson*) I hope you know what you're doing with that girl.

HANSON. Oh, definitely. (*He moves* R *below the sofa*)

JOAN. Better leave him alone, Maureen.

MAUREEN (*moving* L *of the sofa and below it to Hanson*) He needs reminding.

HANSON. On whose authority, Miss Wilkinson?

MAUREEN. Those people who hire you to educate the . . .

HANSON. That's their fault for serving up dishes like her. We're not sticks of chalk.

MAUREEN. I never said you were.

HANSON. So put that over your shoulder and start marching.

(*There is a cry from the kitchen and the sound of breaking glass.* JOAN *rushes out down* L)

Relax, Maureen. Relax.

ARNIE (*moving* L *of Maureen; cheerfully*) *Relax.*

MAUREEN. I am relaxed. There's a question of behaviour, isn't there?

HANSON. My behaviour's strictly human.

ARNIE. It's strictly human.

HANSON. Or are you against that, too?

ARNIE (*moving up* C) Are you against that, too?

HANSON (*to Arnie*) What's the matter with you?

(JOAN *enters* L)

JOAN. One broken glass, that's all. (*She moves up* LC)

(SHEILA *enters* L *with a tray of glasses*)

SHEILA (*moving* R) I broke a glass! (*She puts the tray on the coffee-table*)

HANSON (*moving* L *of the coffee-table*) Right, then. (*He starts pouring out the drinks*)

ARNIE (*moving above the sofa; to Maureen*) What's got *into* you?

MAUREEN. What?
HANSON. Joan? Maureen? A little for you, Sheila?

(SHEILA *takes her drink and wanders round room, above sofa, inspecting trophies, etc.*)

JOAN. I'll have a glassful . . . (*She sits on the chair* C)
HANSON. But certainly.
MAUREEN (*moving above the table and pouring tea*) I'll make do with tea.
HANSON. Naturally. (*To Joan*) We have a little whisky here for the menfolk. If you like . . .
JOAN. Oh, beer will do.
HANSON. And Arnold.

(ARNIE *takes his glass of whisky from Hanson*)

JOAN. Don't give him whisky. (*Rising*) One glass knocks him off his feet. (*She goes to Hanson for her drink*)
HANSON. Aha!

(ARNIE *downs his whisky in one swallow*)

JOAN. I've warned you. (*She moves above the sofa*)

(HANSON *tots up Arnie's glass again, and* ARNIE *drinks it off.* ARNIE *screws his face, holds his stomach, then his head, gesticulates with violent, staccatic motions, lurches erratically one way then another, goes boss-eyed, knock-kneed, etc.*)

All right. All right.

(ARNIE *stands motionless in the centre of the room*)

(HANSON (*expressionless*) Oh dear. Oh dear, I haven't laughed so much for ages. Are you sure you're old enough, Sheila?
SHEILA (*returned, after tour of inspection, to coffee-table, by Hanson*) Course I am.
HANSON. I meant for alcohol, my dear. (*He slaps his thigh*) Oh, my!
ARNIE. My *friends*!
HANSON. *What?*
ARNIE. I would like to address you, if I may.
HANSON (*standing by the coffee-table*) Oh.

(ARNIE *wanders below the sofa.* JOAN *moves* L *of the sofa.* MAUREEN *moves* L *and closes the kitchen door*)

ARNIE (*after a brief hesitation*) This—celebration—is not an ordinary celebration. Oh, you may say, it *looks* an ordinary celebration. And I admit. It has all the signs, the characteristics, all the moeurs, as they say in German. Of a celebration. But the fact is . . . What? What? (*He looks round questioningly*)
JOAN. Is that the end? (*She moves above the sofa*)
ARNIE. I have always in my life attempted to deal—fairly, with my fellow men.

HANSON (*indicating Sheila*) And women.

ARNIE. Ah. (*He holds up an admonitory finger*) And it would, indeed, be mealy-mouthed . . .

HANSON. It would.

ARNIE (*moving between the sofa and the chair* C) Of me. Ungracious. Prevaricating. (*Moving down* R) To let you assume that this is merely a celebration. This is, in fact . . . What is this? (*He holds up his glass*)

(HANSON *holds up the whisky bottle to Arnie*)

HANSON. One of the very worst brands, old friend.

ARNIE (*wipes his hand, surprised, across his forehead*) I'm *sweating*.

JOAN. I told you he'd fall down.

MAUREEN. Perhaps we better put on the music and calm down.

ARNIE (*moving* C) An event of such gigantic proportions as to be virtually invisible to the naked human eye! It is . . . Do they wash up in this?

HANSON (*totting up Arnie's glass*) Only one of the minor rituals of distillation. Why, I could tell you . . .

JOAN. We'll have that another time.

ARNIE. I want *all* of you. (*Moving below the sofa* L) I want all of you to be content. This evening I want you to remember—I want you to remember I want you. (*He sits* L *on the sofa*)

HANSON. What?

ARNIE. What?

HANSON. Well, if not "what", then "why"?

ARNIE. I don't want to know why. Any damn fool can give you reasons *why*. All I'm interested in is how. Why is a kind of sentimentality I heartily eschew. I *eschew* IT. Why is of no more interest to me than *when*. You can put why and when into—wherever you'd like to put them, and blow them to smithereens, for me.

HANSON. God! A religious maniac!

ARNIE. I want an evening of—ease, of peace, of relaxation. The— *flow* of gentle laughter, conversation—the natural intimacy between friends.

JOAN (L *of sofa*) I'd like to recite a poem.

ARNIE. What?

HANSON. Oh, steady, Joan.

JOAN. I think I shall.

ARNIE (*pained*) You're being revolting—I said the *natural* flow of conversation, not a poem.

JOAN. You said the flow.

MAUREEN. Yes. You did say the flow.

(JOAN *begins to recite*)

HANSON (*crossing to Sheila with a bottle*) Have another drink, Sheila.

SHEILA. Oh, ta.

(HANSON *fills Sheila's glass*)

HANSON. You are enjoying yourself?

(HANSON *returns down* R)

SHEILA. Oh, super!

(JOAN *recites, at first her fingers holding her cheeks, then, as she goes on, growing more confident*)

JOAN.   I saw love passing by my window
          Early one morning on a lightsome day . . .
ARNIE. Oh, no.
HANSON. Joan . . .
JOAN.   Its face was warm and its look so hopeful
          And pleasure and happiness in its features lay.

(ARNIE *covers his face with embarrassment*)

ARNIE. Oh, no. (*Groaning*) This can't go on.
HANSON. Joan, my dear, dear girl . . .
SHEILA. No. Sir, it's super!
MAUREEN (*moving* C) No, let her go on. (*She sits in the chair* C)

(*For a moment they argue over this,* SHEILA *and* MAUREEN *attempting to quieten the other two. Meanwhile* JOAN *carries on reciting*)

JOAN (*moving* L *of the sofa*) I saw love hurrying in the meadow,
          Its steps so light over the leaden clay,
          Its breath was quick and its voice beseeching
          And I heard its cries as I fled away.

(ARNIE *rises and moves to the radiogram, making noises*)

          I saw love sitting in a cottage,
          About its feet did children play,
          Their sounds were loud, their voices lusty,
          And I saw love smile to see them gay.

(*As* JOAN *continues to recite, the others gradually grow quiet, turning to listen to her*)

          I saw love bending with the sickle,
          Though all the thorns were clustered in its way,
          Its body aged and its head now shaking,
          And with the wind it seemed to sway.

          I saw love trudging by my window
          Late one evening on a darksome day,
          Its face was worn and its look despairing
          And grief and sorrow on its features lay.

          I saw love carried to the graveside
          The day was sunny and the month was May;
          Across its brow was a wreath of laurel
          And in its hands a clean white spray.

(*For a moment everyone is silent and still*)

HANSON. Oh, I say. That's very good.

MAUREEN. Lovely.

SHEILA. It was super, miss.

HANSON. No, I really do think that was very good.

(*Everyone is a little awed. Then* ARNIE *moves abruptly*)

ARNIE (*moving down* L; *suddenly*)

> There was a young woman of Leeds
> Who swallowed a packet of seeds,
> She grew peas on her chest,
> Runner beans in her vest,
> And all round her kneecaps grew weeds.

HANSON. There was a young man of Bangkok . . .

MAUREEN (*rising*) No! (*She moves to the sofa*)

ARNIE. Oh, I say . . .

(SHEILA *rises and moves to the bookcase up* L)

HANSON. Who swallowed a musical clock:

> He could play a toccata,

(MAUREEN *sits* C *on the sofa.* SHEILA *moves above the sofa.* ARNIE *moves above the chair* C)

> Chopin's Moonlight Sonata.
> By simply removing his sock.

(JOAN *moves to the chair* C *and sits*)

ARNIE. Oh . . . This is the happiest day of my life. I want you to know that . . . Revelations are simply pouring from the skies! Sheila! (*He sits on the* R *arm of Joan's chair and puts his arm round her*)

HANSON. Sheila, what contribution could you make, my dear?

ARNIE. A few hand stands might cause a stir. Perhaps some extraordinary gymnastic feats acquired at the hands of Miss Wilkinson.

HANSON. You can commit poetry, my dear. We—we can merely recite it.

SHEILA. You've forgotten to give sir his telegram, sir.

HANSON. Telegram? Telegram?

JOAN. Telegram?

HANSON. Ah . . .

ARNIE (*totally bemused, his arm still warmly about Joan*) I once read somewhere in a novel, perhaps . . .

HANSON. Scott!

ARNIE. Scott!

HANSON. That's his name! (*He points to the door*)

MAUREEN. Whose?

HANSON (*sitting* R *of Maureen on the sofa*) You remember Scott! A tall, lanky boy who wore glasses and dirty teeth. Won the long jump one year, I believe, by simply falling on his head.

(SHEILA *sits on the* R *arm of the sofa*)

ARNIE. Oh, Scott! Wasn't he the boy . . .

HANSON. Could contain himself no longer during a mathematics lesson and furtively urinated out of an upper window when he presumed no-one was looking.

(JOAN *giggles*)

MAUREEN. Now, that's enough.

ARNIE. Brought on a case of Thompson's disease. An hitherto unknown medical syndrome characterized by a sudden staring of the eyes, an energetic raising of the arms, and a loud, screaming sound emitted from between the teeth.

HANSON. It was first witnessed in an elderly caretaker of that name who happened to be passing beneath the window at the time.

(JOAN *breaks out into laughter*, SHEILA *giggles*)

JOAN. Is he *here*?

SHEILA (*attempting to conceal her laughter*) He was.

ARNIE. A remarkable youth, I seem to recollect. Went through all the stages of puberty by the age of eleven. Caused endless consternation amongst the younger boys.

HANSON. As we were emerging from the house, a short while ago, my young companion and I, our course set for the hostelry, whom should we discover on the step but Scott himself, attired in dark uniform and peaked cap. Great Heavens, said I, the police. Whereupon he indicated an insignia on his arm which suggested he was in the employ of the Post Office with special responsibility for the delivery of urgent messages. Thrusting one such into my hand he departed with an alacrity I can only assume was inspired by our past acquaintance. So intoxicated was I by the chatter of my companion that, until this moment, I'm afraid I have quite overlooked it . . . (*He rises, searches his pockets, and finds the telegram. Reading*) Greetings!

JOAN. Is that all it says?

HANSON (*tendentiously*) That's merely the envelope. (*He opens it*)

(ARNIE *rises and moves* C. SHEILA *rises and moves* R)

Ah! This is what Scott has written. Greetings again! Here we are . . . Regret . . . Regret. Regret mother unwell stop cutting holiday short stop hope to make it some other time stop father.

JOAN. What's that?

(HANSON *moves to Joan, gives her the telegram, then moves down* R)

HANSON. Another drink? Maureen?

MAUREEN. I'll have some whisky.

(JOAN *having read the telegram giggles.* ARNIE, *his arm still around her shoulder, gazes into the distance*)

JOAN. I've cleaned every rotten stick in this house. (*To the others*) I've even dusted every rotten piece of dust.

HANSON (*taking Maureen her whisky*) Oh! Oh! Oh! (*He moves back down* R)

JOAN (*rising to* C) There's not a mark nor a sign of life anywhere, and now they've decided not to come. (*She is very pleased, yet apparently, with her giggling, trying to hide her feelings from Arnie*)

ARNIE (*rising and moving to the radiogram*) Now. We are about to dance. (*He switches it on*)

(SHEILA *moves* R *of the coffee-table*)

JOAN. Here. Have you read this? Isn't it marvellous! That really is the best news I've had all day.

(*The music starts*)

ARNIE (*moving to Sheila*) Sheila. Would you escort me about the floor?

(ARNIE *and* SHEILA *dance to down* L)

A limb here, a limb there. One or two gesticulations in unexpected places—and there we are. Ups!

(ARNIE *is unsteady, slow and mechanical, as he manoeuvres* SHEILA *slowly about the room*)

HANSON (*moving above the sofa*) Shall we form a chorus? Surround the principal players with thrashing . . .

JOAN (*to Arnie*) Loved one! Did you hear? Have you seen this? (*She is still giggling, despite herself: for her, now, the evening is a huge success*)

(ARNIE *maintains a stoical indifference, lumbering on down* L)

HANSON (*moving to the radiogram*) Arnie. Show us your armour.

JOAN (*moving to the coffee-table*) We can get rid of that, soon, while we're at it.

HANSON. I know a secret. (*He crosses to the cupboard*)

MAUREEN. What . . .

HANSON. I know a secret!

SHEILA (*laughing*) What is it?

HANSON. Are you ready?

JOAN (*pouring herself a drink*) No rowdy stuff, Hanson.

HANSON. Are you ready? (*He darts to the cupboard, and with a sudden gesture, tries to open it*) Woman! Behold they . . . Oh, it's locked.

JOAN. Don't look at me.

HANSON (*moving above the sofa to the bookcase up* L) Arnold. What is this?

SHEILA. Oh, Arnie. Can't we see it?

ARNIE (*stopping the dance*) What? (*He stares at Sheila in consternation*)

SHEILA (*quietly*) Can't we see it, sir?

ARNIE. Who asked you in here?

HANSON. I did, Robin.

ARNIE. Show her the aeroplane. There's a stuffed eagle over there.

HANSON. Aren't we going to see . . .

ARNIE (*moving* c *below the sofa*) And over there you'll observe a Lee-Enfield rifle, a weapon of historical importance to the British nation.

HANSON. Arnold, if you'll just allow . . .

ARNIE (*moving* LC) With that weapon we preserved . . . (*He gestures airily about him*)

HANSON. Look, I don't wish to get impersonal, old boy.

ARNIE. And what are we now? Gropers in the debris of our . . .

HANSON. Arnold. (*Moving above the sofa*) Do I understand you are about to entertain us?

ARNIE. Tell us, Hanson. How does your mother keep her stockings up?

HANSON. Ooo! Ooo!

(ARNIE *turns off the radiogram and returns* RC)

JOAN. I think that's enough.

MAUREEN. We better quieten down . . .

SHEILA. It's good, miss!

JOAN. If you want something to shout about, there's always this. (*She thrusts the telegram into Arnie's hand*)

ARNIE. It's Hanson. (*He crosses* LC) He's an historical aberration.

HANSON. Oooo!

ARNIE. A turnip!

HANSON. Ooo!

(SHEILA *and* JOAN *giggle*)

ARNIE. A sod.

HANSON (*moving down* C) Ooo! Ooo! You heard him! (*He writes across a large imaginary blackboard*) Tries hard: a willing worker, but effort frequently suffocated in pompous supposition.

(ARNIE *waves his arms about indecisively*)

Ooo! You heard! (*He writes*) Self-indulgent and tends to melodrama when opposed. Suffers from affectations, not least of which a pretension to reality. (*He bows to the room*) Thus write I across all my reports. (*Vaguely facetious*) Loved one.

JOAN (*retaining her drink throughout*) That's enough! (*She sits* R *of Maureen on the sofa*)

ARNIE. It's him. He's a propagator of untruth.

HANSON. Untruth! Why, he's a lie himself. If you measured him by any reality, he'd be invisible. (*He puts his tongue out triumphantly at Arnie*)

ARNIE. That rifle's *loaded*.

(HANSON *pauses, then looks up. He hesitates*)

HANSON. Liar! (*He goes to the sideboard for the rifle*)

MAUREEN (*to Joan*) Is it loaded?

JOAN (*giggling*) I don't know.

MAUREEN (*rising and moving down* R) I think we've had enough of this.

SHEILA. They're only playing, miss!

(HANSON *lifts the rifle down and brings it above the sofa to* C)

ARNIE. May I?

(ARNIE *puts the telegram in his pocket, first one, then the other, as* HANSON *fumbles with the rifle. Then* ARNIE *takes it from him, removes the safety catch and draws back the bolt.* JOAN *rises and moves* L *of Maureen*)

All right. A pretension to reality. (*He raises the rifle and presses it to Hanson's temple. He is still unsteady with drink*) It's loaded.

HANSON (*after a pause; loudly*) Rubbish! (*He giggles*)

ARNIE. I'll fire it.

(HANSON *is silent*)

Well?

HANSON. Trouble-maker, and known disseminator of bad habits.

MAUREEN. That's far enough.

ARNIE. Are you ready?

HANSON. Yes.

(ARNIE *squeezes the trigger*)

JOAN. No!

ARNIE. It's rusty. Hold your head still.

(HANSON *stands tensely, assuming some dignity.* SHEILA *has covered her face up.* ARNIE *holds the rifle more awkwardly to gain further pressure on the trigger. He squeezes again. There is a click.* ARNIE *still holds the rifle as before.* HANSON *laughs*)

MAUREEN. Oh, God! That's enough.

HANSON. Everything, you see. False all the way through. (*He takes the rifle from Arnie, laughing with real pleasure. He points it at Arnie, ramming back the bolt*) Arnold; you're a falsity! (*His laughter suddenly breaks. He looks down at the rifle—examines it*) It is loaded.

ARNIE. Yes.

HANSON (*looking up in horror*) And you pulled the trigger.

ARNIE. Yes.

HANSON. Why! . . . You madman! (*He throws the rifle down on the sofa*)

ARNIE. It was a choice you made on the evidence of your own senses, Jeffrey.

HANSON. You're mad!

ARNIE. That's not true.

HANSON (*moving* RC; *to the women*) He could have killed me!

JOAN (*dismissive*) Fools! You're both fools!

(ARNIE, *swaying, picks up the rifle*)

HANSON. What? (*He suddenly stares at her, drunkenly distracted*) He could have killed me!

ARNIE (*pointing the rifle at Hanson*) As a matter of fact, I still can.

HANSON. No!

JOAN. Arnie!

MAUREEN. No!

(SHEILA *screams*. ARNIE *pulls the trigger, then gazes intrigued at* HANSON's *expression*)

ARNIE. The firing-pin's removed. There's no contact with the cartridge. (*He lowers the rifle*) It can never go off.

(HANSON *grabs the rifle from Arnie*)

HANSON. You know what I think?

ARNIE. You take it too seriously, Big John.

(HANSON *stares at him impotently, blind with rage*)

(*Slowly*) It really is unforgivable, isn't it?

MAUREEN. You better go, Sheila. Did you bring a coat?

HANSON. She's not going.

SHEILA. I don't want to go.

MAUREEN. I think you'd better, girl, and do as you're told this once.

HANSON (*crossing below to Sheila*) I said she's not going! (*He takes Sheila's arm. To Arnie*) God. What a deceiver. It was false, bogus, all the way through. He even makes a virtue of it.

ARNIE (*to Maureen*) Shall we dance?

MAUREEN. You've gone too far, Arnold. I think we'd better go.

HANSON. Go! I think—with all due insolence to our host—that he should be compelled to open his bloody cupboard *door*!

ARNIE. Mockery ill becomes you.

HANSON. I think he should . . .

(ARNIE *throws the rifle under the sofa*)

ARNIE (*with assumed, drunken dignity*) *You* think? Your thoughts, Hanson—they're superfluous here. And your insolence undistinguished. You've been revealed as a pompous boor. Your otiose circumlocutions no longer sufficient to conceal the cringing, shivering coward within; your boldest gestures about as revelationary as a flea's. Do you really believe that I'm under any obligation to reveal *my* soul to you? My weaknesses stand higher than your greatest virtues.

MAUREEN. That's enough, for God's sake.

ARNIE. My only regret is, out of past charity, I have such weak substances on which to wreak my revenge.

HANSON (*applauding*) Oh, bravo. Bravo.

ARNIE (*moving to the hall door*) I regret it all. All this. It's too puny for contempt!

JOAN (*moving below the sofa*) Where are you going?

ARNIE. What?

JOAN. These people: you *invited* them.

(ARNIE *comes back and takes the whisky bottle from the table*)

ARNIE. Assume they aren't here. It's an easier alternative to assuming that they are. (*He returns towards the hall door*)
JOAN (*as Arnie crosses below her; with curiosity*) Have you read that telegram?

(ARNIE *pauses*, L *of Joan*)

In your pocket.
ARNIE. I heard.

(*Pause*)

JOAN. They're not coming. As long as you realize that when you wake up. And it's just as well they aren't. You're blind drunk.
ARNIE. Do you know what you're saying? (*He snatches at his pockets, searching for, then finding the telegram*) I know what it says! I heard! (*To Hanson*) Did you say that Scott wrote this? He wants firing! Did *he* write this? Then sack him! He's no good. Did I tell you what he did to Thompson?
JOAN (*moving between the sofa and the chair* C) You better go to bed.
ARNIE. I am! I am! (*He stares at them, maddened, full of threat*) I am!

(ARNIE *goes to the hall door, stumbles, regains his balance, and exits*)

HANSON. So's friendship, if not love, repaid;
         And by a graceless hand is trust betrayed.
MAUREEN (*moving to the sofa*) Stop it! I've had enough! All this indulgence. (*She sits* R *on the sofa*)
HANSON (*going above the sofa to the cupboard*) Well, that comes out at least. (*He tries to wrench the cupboard door open, then kicks the thin wood open*) Why, it's empty! There's nothing here! (*He turns round, broken by his rage, and moves down* R) He must have it up there with him.
JOAN. Just look what you've done . . . (*She giggles*)
SHEILA (*moving in* LC) He's jealous.
JOAN. What?
SHEILA. It's because he's jealous. That's why he's gone . . .
MAUREEN (*rising*) Sheila!
SHEILA. He is. He's jealous of Mr Hanson. Anybody can see.

(JOAN *is more disillusioned than annoyed*)

JOAN (*passively*) Oh, for goodness' sake. (*Moving to* L *of Maureen*) Get her out.
SHEILA. He is!
JOAN (*almost indifferently*) Get out.
MAUREEN. Go on, Sheila. Go on. You'd better go now. (*To Hanson*) Take her out.

(HANSON *moves below* R *of Sheila*)

SHEILA. He is! You're all jealous. All of you.
JOAN (*passively*) Take her out for goodness' sake.

(MAUREEN *takes Joan's arm as her violence grows*)

MAUREEN (*to Hanson*) You'd better go.

(HANSON *takes Sheila's arm*)

HANSON (*taking Sheila to the hall door*) All right. All right. But don't blame her. That camel up there. Now you just shout at him.

(HANSON *and* SHEILA *exit to the hall, leaving the door open.* JOAN *stands tensely,* MAUREEN *holding her until the front door slams*)

JOAN (*quietly*) I'll have to wait for my mother. She should have been back by now. That girl.
MAUREEN. I'll stay a little longer.
JOAN. Would you? Do you mind? It's very kind of you.
MAUREEN (*sitting* R *on the sofa*) We might as well sit down.

(JOAN *wanders down* L, *then above the chairs to* C)

JOAN. That girl.
MAUREEN. I shouldn't worry.
JOAN. Isn't it quiet? It must be late. (*She pauses*) She can't be long. Everything must be shut by now. (*She moves up* C)
MAUREEN. Will Arnold have gone to bed?
JOAN. Oh . . . (*She listens*) We won't see him again tonight. (*She pauses*) I've been dreading having a scene with my mother this evening while people were here. That's why I asked her to go out.
MAUREEN. Asked her?
JOAN (*moving above the sofa*) I told her this evening that she would have to leave. Go and live somewhere else . . . It sounds hard. But there was no other way of doing it. Believe me. (*She moves down* LC)
MAUREEN. Is that what Arnold was in a mood about? I mean, when we came.
JOAN. No. No. He doesn't know I've told her yet. (*She moves down* L *and back*)

(MAUREEN *watches* JOAN *moving listlessly about the room*)

I had to tell her to go, you know. (*She pauses*) I've never seen her so hurt. Never. She—I've never seen her so hurt.
MAUREEN. Where will she go when she leaves?
JOAN (*sitting* L *on the sofa*) She's grown so attached to Arnie. (*After a pause*) Don't you think it's strange? The way he's always surrounded by women?
MAUREEN. Women?
JOAN. I don't know. He can't bear to be in this house alone. Can you imagine that? Don't you think it's extraordinary? (*She pauses*) You should see the look of relief on his face when I come in. Or my mother comes in. And he's sitting here alone. I don't think he's even aware of it. (*She gets up, moves round again, restlessly, to down* L, *then*

round the chairs to C) I was like a wild animal when we first got married. Always smashing things. I couldn't put my hand down without knocking something over. I was never still for one minute. (*She sits down again as before*) We were always fighting. You know, fists and things. (*She laughs into her hand*) It's awful, isn't it? But we used just to stand up, bashing each other.

(MAUREEN *laughs*)

I think this drink's beginning to have an effect on me. (*She snorts into her hand*) Have you heard of anybody carrying on like that? I'm glad, actually. That they're not coming tomorrow. (*She looks round at the room*) It was all prepared. All ready. Actually they're very nice. I don't know why. Will you have something else? I'm sure you'd like them. (*She rises*)

MAUREEN. No. I don't think I will.

JOAN. Would you like a stuffed eagle?

MAUREEN. I don't think so. No.

JOAN. A ship?

MAUREEN. No thanks.

JOAN (*moving down* R) It's all yours, if you want it. S'll going out. Sweeping changes. Actually. You mustn't tell anybody about this, will you? (*She puts her glass on the coffee-table*)

MAUREEN. No . . .

JOAN. You promise?

MAUREEN (*nods uncertainly*) Yes.

JOAN (*crossing below to* LC) The fact is, Arnie doesn't give a damn for anybody. I'm exactly the same. Do you know anything about children?

MAUREEN. Well. I teach them.

JOAN (*moving* L *of Maureen*) Ah, yes. (*She looks at Maureen freshly*) Are you religious? You don't mind me asking.

MAUREEN (*pause*) No. Well . . .

JOAN. Do you believe in God?

MAUREEN (*uncertainly*) Well, in a sort of . . .

JOAN (*lifting back her hair*) I honestly don't know what to believe in. Is that the time? You absolutely promise?

MAUREEN. Yes.

JOAN (*sitting on the sofa*) Well, I'll tell you. (*She looks around*) Arnold actually . . .

MAUREEN (*pause*) Yes?

JOAN. Is God.

MAUREEN. Oh.

JOAN. He's only assumed the identity of a schoolteacher in order to remain incognito. Inconspicuous. For a God, you see, who believes in modesty and self-effacement there are severe doctrinal problems in asserting that he's God at all. Do you understand what I mean?

(JOAN *watches Maureen for a moment with some satisfaction.* MAUREEN *gives no reply at all*)

It's an enormous privilege, of course. (*She pauses*) Being married to
him at all.

(Mrs Ellis *appears in the hall doorway.* Maureen *seeing her, rises
immediately*)

Maureen. Oh!

(Joan *turns dreamily, slowly, as she sees* Maureen's *reaction.* Mrs
Ellis's *appearance is dreadful: dressed in men's pyjamas, she has a bottle
in her hand. Her look is compounded of many feelings: possessiveness,
triumph, greed. Her matronly breasts are scarcely concealed by the jacket,
and as she sways to between the sofa and the chair* c, *the vision changes to
that of a besotted old lady. For a moment* Joan *fails to grasp what she
sees. When she does, it is with a cry of denial like a child's*)

Joan. Mam! (*She staggers to her feet*) Mother.
Mrs Ellis. Do you know . . .
Joan. Mam!
Mrs Ellis. It's not in there. Not in there—as we all thought. (*She
indicates the cupboard*) It's not in there at all. He's hidden it—would
you believe it, the cunning devil?—he's hidden it under the bed!
Joan. No. No.
Mrs Ellis (*to Maureen*) Underneath! Well! Whoever said he
wasn't cunning!
Joan. You . . .
Mrs Ellis. It's all lies. Everything. You—you . . . The things
he told me. You said he wanted me to go. You did. In fact, it wasn't
that he wanted at all.
Joan. What?
Mrs Ellis. Arnie.
Joan. Oh, no—no . . .
Mrs Ellis (*moving below the chair down* lc) You ask him.
Joan. Oh, God. No. (*She sinks down on the sofa, burying her face in
her hands*)
Mrs Ellis. Well. Well, then—who's sorry now? (*She collapses
dazedly into the chair down* lc) Are we having a party? Who's this,
then? Another of Arnie's friends?

Curtain

ACT III

Scene i

SCENE—*The same. The next morning.*

When the CURTAIN *rises, the window-curtains are still closed and the room in semi-darkness. The armour, in pieces, is lying in a pile on sacking between the sofa and the chair* C, *with the sword and eagle on top.* JOAN *is discovered with pan and brush, sweeping the floor between the armchairs. She moves up* C, *draws the window-curtains and opens the windows. She goes to the coffee-table down* R, *picks up some empty bottles and puts them into a large box above the kitchen door. She then sweeps near the pile of armour.* ARNIE *appears in the doorway up* L, *tousled, genial, his shirt unbuttoned. He yawns, stretches, smacks his lips and looks round.* JOAN *goes on working.*

ARNIE (*in the doorway*) Well. Well. Shipshape. Someone has been up early, I can see.

JOAN (*crossing below the sofa to the coffe-table*) I've made coffee. Is that all right?

ARNIE. Ah. Fine. Fine. (*He comes slowly into the room*)

JOAN. I haven't cooked anything. I didn't think anyone would feel like eating. (*She sweeps by the coffee-table*)

ARNIE (*sitting* L *of the table*) Quite true. Quite true. (*He comes to the table, looks round at the various objects on it*) Well, well, well. That was a very frivolous evening, Joan. All that booze. We shan't go through that again. Not for a very long time. No, we shan't. We certainly shan't. What? We shan't. (*He yawns, snaps his mouth shut. Suddenly he shadows boxes, briefly, quickly. Then he yawns again, stretches*) I've got to get down to weight. This is getting embarrassing. Last fight I ever had I only weighed three stone ten. No, was it four? (*He gazes at Joan, then, after a while, quietly sings*)

> Come ye thankful people come
> Raise the song of harvest home,
> All is safely gathered in
> Ere the winter storms begin;
> God our Maker doth provide
> For our wants to be supplied;
> Come to God's own temple, come:
> Raise the song of harvest home.
> Where's Edie then?

JOAN. She hasn't got up yet. (*She crosses to the box, tips the pan into it, crosses* R *to the cupboard, puts the pan and brush in it, then moves down and sits* R *on the sofa*)

ARNIE. The fact is, I feel in a very philosophic frame of mind. All my life I've looked for some positive reaction in people. Did you know that? It's amazing what human initiative will rise to once it sets itself to a particular task. (*He rises and moves* L *of the sofa. Continuing absently*) When I was a boy we had a milkman who came in a horse and trap. He wore a little bowler hat and a striped apron and came in each morning from the country with cans of fresh milk and ladled it all out with little ladles. Beautiful. They went up from one the size of a thimble to one as big as his hat. He ran over a boy one day. The wheel of his cart went over his head. It wasn't his fault. But he offered the boy's mother free milk for a year; you know, for goodwill and neighbourliness. She was very poor. She had eleven children. I don't think he knew that at the time. (*He pauses*) He went out of business in six months. Bankrupt. (*He pauses*) You should have seen this woman's house. Milk, there was, everywhere. Nothing but milk.

(JOAN *rises, goes to the table, picks up the coffee-pot, and exits to the kitchen.* ARNIE *talks through to her*)

You know, I've always had the ambition to be a writer. The things I'd write about would be fairly rhetorical in manner. Subjects—well, it may even have caught your attention.

(JOAN *enters and stands in the doorway*)

The extraordinary mixture of hysteria and passivity one gets in society today. (*He moves below the sofa* R) I mean . . .

(MRS ELLIS *appears in the door from the hall. She is carrying a small suitcase and is dressed in a coat and hat, a small fur round her shoulders*)

MRS ELLIS. I'll send for my things when I've got an address.
JOAN (*moving to the table*) You'd better put the case down . . .
ARNIE. I thought there for a moment, you know, that we were going off on holiday. God, weather like this, too. It's incomprehensible.
JOAN (*ignoring him*) I'm heating up the coffee.

(MRS ELLIS *stands gazing irresolutely round her.* ARNIE *sits on the sofa*)

And do take that coat off. You'll be roasted alive. The pot's ready to fetch through. (*She busies herself rearranging the table*)
MRS ELLIS. Joan . . .
JOAN. All it requires is lifting.

(MRS ELLIS *exits to the kitchen*)

ARNIE. This is quite extraordinary. I've forgotten his name now. But this boy fell off the school roof on—Friday, it must have been. Over forty feet in height. No. I'm wrong there. Nearer fifty. Fell like a stone. Bang. Right on his head. By every right it should have killed him. But no. This should interest you, Edie. He's scarcely hit the ground than he stands up and says, "Sir, I didn't fall. Somebody pushed me." So damned anxious, in wandering near the parapet, to show he hadn't broken a rule.

(MRS ELLIS *appears in the kitchen doorway, looking lost*)

MRS ELLIS. I don't seem able to find it.

JOAN. Look for it, Mother. Put the light on. Open the curtain.

MRS ELLIS. Yes . . .

JOAN. And do take your coat off.

MRS ELLIS (*moving* C) Yes . . . (*She starts back, falters*) I don't know how you can just sit there.

ARNIE. Sit?

MRS ELLIS. I can hardly stand!

ARNIE. Now then. Now then. There's no need to get upset.

MRS ELLIS. Upset! (*She buries her face in her hands*)

JOAN. It's all right, Mother.

MRS ELLIS (*moving* LC; *moaning*) I don't know what to do.

JOAN (*moving* R *of Mrs Ellis*) You'll stay here, Mother. It's all right.

MRS ELLIS. Oh, Joan—Joan!

JOAN (*helping Mrs Ellis slowly towards the hall*) Now, you're all right. You're all right.

(MRS ELLIS *cries into her hands*)

ARNIE (*brightly*) How about some coffee?

JOAN. Come on. You'd better come upstairs. I'll help you up.

MRS ELLIS. Oh, God, Joan. What am I going to do?

JOAN. Oh, now. You come up. Come on, now. Come on.

MRS ELLIS. I can't. I can't.

JOAN. I'll bring you something up. Now, come on. You'll be all right.

(JOAN *and* MRS ELLIS *exit to the hall and stairs.* ARNIE *rises and moves to the window, putting his hands in his pockets and whistling*)

ARNIE (*moving above the sofa*) This is quite extraordinary. (*He touches some imaginary person's arm*) About two days ago the Director of Education came up to me and said, "Bancroft", he said—I mean it's not as if my name was Bancroft—"Bancroft, I don't know quite how to tell you this, and I should hate it to get around. But the fact is, Bancroft, my wife has recently begun to manufacture money. The thing is, that periodically she lowers her knickers and from inside takes out a miscellaneous collection of coins. The process, as far as I am aware, Bancroft, has completely taken over her excretory organs. And it's mostly silver. The coins, I mean." You know—would you believe it—the only comment he made after telling me all this was "Pity it isn't gold, Bancroft. Just like that rotten bitch to produce second best." (*He laughs and moves upstage*)

(JOAN *enters*)

Anyway, I thought you'd like to know.

(JOAN *crosses to the sideboard for a glass*)

Oh, how is the old bird?

(Joan *returns to* l *of the sofa*)

(*Moving below the sofa* r) You know, this unnerves me (*Sitting on the sofa*) I'm looking for some sort of constructive attitude from you, Joan. Something a bit bolder. To generalize about one's misfortune is invariably a sign of moral recovery in my book. If you could work something up on those lines I'd be immensely grateful.

Joan. Yes. (*She moves down* l)

Arnie. I think I need to feel degenerate.

Joan. I'm taking my mother up a glass of milk.

(Joan *exits to the kitchen*)

Arnie. You see, they're not the sort of remarks I'm looking for, Joan. The sort I'm looking for only you can provide. There's no one else. My only other opportunity for being punished lies immobilized, apparently, upstairs.

(Joan *enters and moves to the table for the sugar*)

Joan. There's an old woman up there, broken in two. (*Crosses back to the kitchen door*)

Arnie. Well, at least she has that reassurance. What have I got? Nothing. Nothing. I don't understand it. I don't. I get no crumb of consolation from this at all. I feel I should get something. I deserve to suffer something, Joan. Even if it's only retribution.

(Joan *has not answered*)

These silences unnerve me. At any moment I'm going to suffer a relapse. I think I should warn you, Joan. You know what that might lead to.

(Joan *still offers no answer*)

(*Suddenly*) I should also like it to be known that this sudden and alarming capacity to behave like a frog—to bespatter detachment on every side, to spawn ill-humour, to sit for hours on end on a pad of disaffection—that all these qualities, while adding conviction to your image as a woman, in no way, *in no way*, improve your image as a man!

(Joan *still makes no sign. Silence*)

(*Indicating the armour, etc.*) I don't understand. Some blame for my predicament attaches itself to you. I lie here, caught up in a million abominations, attributes, some of them fed in long before concep-tion. And some of them, *some of them*, fed in by you! In that clammy little hand lie parts of me I don't think, in all honesty, you under-stand. (*He rises and moves to Joan at the kitchen door*) Guilt and austerity are not necessary compatible, Joan. I mean—effusiveness could make your message just as clear.

Joan. You've behaved like a dwarf. Everything in your life is like that. Dwarfish.

ARNIE. Well. Yes. That's something.

(JOAN *exits to the kitchen.* ARNIE *talks through the door to her*)

A dwarf. (*He pauses, reflecting*) I don't like that, somehow. (*He half laughs*) You know I object to that, Joan. I don't feel like a dwarf. (*He looks at his hands*) I wouldn't describe them particularly, for instance, as dwarfish. (*After a pause*) Haven't you anything else to say?

(JOAN *enters* L *with a glass of milk*)

JOAN (*in the doorway*) What are you going to do, Arnie?
ARNIE. I don't know—I'll do the only decent thing, I suppose.
JOAN. Yes.
ARNIE. That's all there is to do.
JOAN. Yes.
ARNIE. I'll marry her.

(*For a moment they are silent*)

JOAN. Why don't you leave, Arnie? And rid yourself of all this torment?
ARNIE (*abstracted*) I don't know. Life has no dignity, Joan. No, I do agree with that. (*He pauses*) And death hasn't a great deal to recommend it, either. (*He pauses*) Both of them when you look at it. They're pretty anonymous affairs. I don't know. I feel I should be able to do something. Isn't there anything you can think of? I feel, you know, the moment's come—it's actually arrived. (*He grasps the air*) And yet it refuses to—emanate. (*Suddenly he looks round at the room*) Anyway, I couldn't leave all this. My own fireside. I've worked hard for all this. I have. It's mine. This is my situation in life.

(JOAN, *after watching him with some attention, turns and moves to the door up* L)

Perhaps I could go mad. Insanity, you know, is the one refuge I've always felt I was able to afford. The insights that irrationality brings. Well, in the end, that's what we're looking for. Cleavages. Cracks. Fissures. Openings. Some little aperture of warmth and light.

(JOAN, *after some hesitation, exits with her glass of milk, closing the door*)

Look, this is a very poor arrangement. I haven't got your attention at all. (*He turns away*) I don't know. I might as well be talking to the wall. (*He rises and goes* R *to the coffee-table, then slowly moves round the walls as if carefully selecting the right spot for his task, rubbing his hand over the surface. Eventually he takes up a stance by the bookcase up* LC)

When I was young, my mother said to me;
"Never drown but in the sea—
Rivers streams and other dilatory courses
Are not contingent with the elemental forces
Which govern you and me—and occasionally your father—

So remember, even if the means are insufficient, rather
Than die in pieces subside by preference as a whole
For disintegration is inimical to the soul
Which seeks the opportunity or the chances
To die in the circumstances
Of a prince, a saviour, or a messiah—
Or something, perhaps, even a little higher—
You and me and several of your aunties,
On my side, though working class, have destinies
Scarcely commensurate with our upbringing;
I hope in you we are instilling
This sense of secret dignities and rights
—Not like your father's side, the lights
Of which I hope we'll never see again,
Who have, I'm afraid, wet blotting paper for a brain! (*He pauses*)
Please, please, my son,
Don't fail me like your father done."

(*He stands for a moment regarding the wall, expectantly, tensed. Then slowly he relaxes. His head sinks. His shoulders droop. His forehead leans against the wall*)

Oh. Oh. Oh.
When I was young, when I was young,
There were so many things I should have done.

The Lights *fade to a Blackout*

SCENE 2

Scene—*The same. Evening, a few days later.*

When the lights come up, the room is empty. A large vase of flowers stands on the table r, *and another on the sideboard. The hall door is open, and from outside the front door comes the sound of voices*)

Hanson (*off; sounding apprehensive and tentative*) Arnie? (*He pauses*) Arnie? Arnie! (*He waits again*) He can't be there. (*He whistles*)
Maureen (*off*) Arnie? (*She knocks*) Can't hear anybody.

(*The front door opens and* Hanson *puts his head round*)

Hanson. No. No-one here. (*He whistles*) No.

(Hanson *and* Maureen *enter the hall and move into the room, shutting both doors.* Hanson *carries a parcel.* Hanson *moves* c, Maureen *down* l)

Maureen. Goodness.
Hanson. I say. (*They look round at the changes*) Drastic renovations, what?
Maureen. Joan?

HANSON. I say . . . (*He whistles a tune to himself as he looks round, tapping furniture and empty spaces with his stick*)
MAUREEN (*opening the kitchen door*) Joan? No: no-one. (*She shrugs*)
HANSON. Well, then . . .
MAUREEN. I suppose we'd better wait. (*She sits down* LC)
HANSON (*moving above the sofa, looking at his watch*) I don't know. What? Arnie! I say. Cupboard restored. Would you believe it? Ship deserted, what?

(*The front door is heard to open.* HANSON *puts the parcel on the table and hastily composes himself, adjusts his tie, etc.* MAUREEN *rises and moves up* L. MRS ELLIS, *carrying a basket, enters and moves above the chair* C)

MRS ELLIS. Oh . . .
MAUREEN. Mrs Ellis . . .
HANSON. We . . . Oh, allow me . . . (*He offers to take her basket*)
MRS ELLIS. No—it's all right.
MAUREEN. We found the door open. We knocked, but there was no-one here.
MRS ELLIS. Oh . . .
MAUREEN. Is Joan out, too?
MRS ELLIS. Yes—I've just been—she—I'll just put these in the kitchen.
HANSON. Please. Allow me. (*He offers to take her basket*)
MRS ELLIS (*moving below the chairs to* L) No. No, it's all right.

(MRS ELLIS *exits into the kitchen*)

HANSON. Well, well . . . (*He whistles a tune again, glances at his watch, then at Maureen, then moves down* R)

(MAUREEN *goes to the kitchen door*)

MAUREEN. How is Arnie, Mrs Ellis?

(*After a moment* MRS ELLIS *comes out*)

MRS ELLIS (*moving below Maureen to* LC) Oh, he's—all right.
HANSON. Fine. Fine. We—popped round. He hasn't been to school. The past few days.
MRS ELLIS. No. (*She takes off her coat*)
HANSON. We . . . ah . . . Thought we'd pop round.
MRS ELLIS (*moving up* L) Yes.
HANSON. Fine. Fine.

(MRS ELLIS *exits to the hall with her coat, closing the door.* HANSON *and* MAUREEN *exchange glances.* HANSON *whistles a tune.* MAUREEN *moves below the sofa.* JOAN *is heard entering the hall*)

MRS ELLIS (*off*) Oh, it's you. Visitors.
JOAN (*off*) What?
MRS ELLIS (*off*) Mr Hanson . . . Schoolteacher . . .

(Hanson *re-composes himself. A moment later* Joan *comes in*)

Joan (*moving above the chair* c) Oh, hello.

Hanson. Joan.

Maureen. And how are you?

Joan. I'm well. Fine. And you?

Maureen. Yes. Fine.

Hanson. Fine. Fine.

Joan. Isn't Arnie in?

Maureen. We knocked, and shouted.

(Mrs Ellis *enters from the hall and goes into the kitchen*)

Hanson. Found the door ajar. What? No answer.

Maureen. No.

Joan (*taking off her coat and putting it in the hall*) If the door was open, he can't be far away.

Hanson. Well, then . . . (*He hesitates*) Everything in order, then?

Joan. I think so. More or less.

Hanson. Well, then . . . (*He glances at his watch*) I suppose we'd better be making tracks.

Joan (*moving down* c) Stay and have some tea if you like.

Hanson. Yes. Fine. Well.

Joan. My mother will be making some.

Hanson. Fine. Fine.

Maureen (*sitting on the sofa*) How is Arnie, Joan?

Joan. I don't know. All right. (*She shrugs*)

Hanson. We were just remarking. Several days since he put in an appearance, what? At school.

Joan. Yes.

Hanson. Nothing to worry about, then?

Joan. No. I don't think so.

(Arnie *appears in the hall, from the stairs. His head is done up, turban-fashion, in a towel. In his hand he carries the sword*)

Hanson. Good. Good. We were just remarking. Vast changes. What?

Joan. What?

Hanson (*turning to the flowers on the coffee-table*) The room.

Joan (*moving down* r *to Hanson*) Ah, yes.

Hanson. Flowers! (*He smells them*) Beautiful.

Joan. Yes. (*She moves upstage a pace*)

Hanson. Altogether. (*He indicates room*) Lighter.

(Arnie *steps into the doorway*)

Joan. Yes.

(*In glancing round* Hanson *and* Joan *become slowly aware of Arnie. There is a moment of silence*)

ARNIE. The King, though broken by his plight,
     Shall rise again to set things right!

(JOAN *moves up* R)

HANSON. Oh . . .
MAUREEN. Arnie . . .
ARNIE (*moving above the sofa*) Well, well, well. How are we all?
Jeff?
HANSON (*moving above the sofa to meet Arnie*) I'm fine. Fine.
ARNIE (*over the sofa back*) And Maureen. How are you, my dear?
MAUREEN (*rising*) I'm well, Arnie. (*She moves above the* C *chair*)
ARNIE. Just arrived, eh?
HANSON. Yes. Yes. Just about.

(JOAN *moves down* R)

ARNIE. Thought I heard sounds. Couldn't be too sure. Got both
my damned ears fastened up.
MAUREEN. And how are you, Arnie, yourself?
ARNIE. Oh, not so bad. Not so bad. Can't grumble. Can't com-
plain.
HANSON. The Head sends his felicitations, Arnie.
ARNIE. Fine. Fine.
HANSON. And the staff and pupils likewise. Looking forward,
needless to say, to your early return to duties.
ARNIE. Ah, yes.
HANSON. Brought a few essentials here, Arnie. (*He indicates the*
parcel) Keep the system mobile, mind alert.
ARNIE. Ah, yes!

(*Silence*)

HANSON. We were just remarking.
ARNIE. Yes.
HANSON. Vast changes since we were here last.
ARNIE. Ah. Changes.
HANSON. The room . . .
ARNIE. Gave them all to the refuse men, you know.
JOAN (*crossing below to* L) I'll just see about the tea.

(JOAN *exits to the kitchen*)

ARNIE (*to Maureen*) And how are you?
MAUREEN. I'm well, Arnie. (*She moves to the radiogram*)
ARNIE. I suppose you've seen their lorry? They have a blade in
the back which crushes them all up. (*Suddenly, hugely*) Crush!
Crush! Crush!
HANSON. What, all of them, old boy?
ARNIE. Absolutely. (*He gestures at the room*) The lot. (*After a*
moment, swinging the sword) 'Cept this, of course!
HANSON. Yes.

ARNIE. I kept it back. (*He whistles between his teeth as, in demonstration, he slashes it about him, moving between the sofa and* C *chair to down* L)

HANSON. Ah, yes. (*He moves to the door up* L)

ARNIE. Bound to come in useful.

HANSON. Yes.

ARNIE. At least, so I thought.

HANSON. Ah, yes, old boy.

ARNIE (*moving* RC) Arms, hands, feet, legs, abdomen. The lot. (*He mimes the lorry's blade*) Head! (*He gurgles, his hand across his throat*)

HANSON (*moving above the chair* C) We spoke to Sheila, by the way.

ARNIE. Yes?

HANSON. Had a little word in her ear.

ARNIE. Ah, yes.

MAUREEN. I think she'll show a little discretion.

ARNIE. She will?

HANSON. I think so, old man.

ARNIE. Good, good. I could do with a little bit of that myself. (*He laughs*) Joan? (*He looks round, he gestures towards the kitchen*) She has a job.

MAUREEN. Oh.

ARNIE. Out to work each day.

HANSON. Yes?

ARNIE. Perhaps she mentioned it?

MAUREEN (*shaking her head*) No. (*She sits down* LC)

ARNIE. She acquired her credentials, I'm glad to say, long before I married her. In a secretarial capacity, of course. (*He sits* L *on the sofa, still holding the sword*)

HANSON. Ah, yes. (*He sits in the chair* C)

ARNIE. Type. Type. Type. You should see her fingers. Flexing. Even in bed.

HANSON. Ah, yes, old boy.

ARNIE. On the other hand . . .

HANSON. Yes, old boy?

ARNIE. Absolutely nothing to worry about.

HANSON. No, no.

ARNIE. The doctor recommends a long sea voyage.

MAUREEN. Sea voyage?

ARNIE. And a complete change of air.

MAURBEN. I see.

ARNIE. I would have thought, myself, that the two of them were perfectly synonymous.

HANSON. Absolutely.

ARNIE. I'm overworked.

HANSON. My dear boy . . .

ARNIE. My nerves, Jeff, are stretched beyond endurance. (*He glances round with some exaggeration to see that he is not overheard*) I'm afraid I should have warned you. Joan . . . (*He taps his head*) You will find her, I'm afraid, considerably changed. Her work—the contingencies of high office, the flow, the rapid, reckless interchange of ideas which has been her lot now—(*Dramatically consulting his bare wrist*)—for the past six hours, leaves her—I'm very much afraid—*prostrate.*

HANSON. Ah, yes.

(JOAN *enters and moves* C)

JOAN. My mother's bringing in the tea.

(ARNIE *moves along the sofa,* JOAN *sits* L *of him*)

HANSON. Oh, that's very kind of you, Joan.

MAUREEN. Shouting at the devils all afternoon. Just one of those ays. When you want a bit of peace you can never get it.

ARNIE. What do you really think, Jeff?

HANSON. Think?

ARNIE. Feel, if you like. What do you really feel?

HANSON. I feel we're completely out of touch with one another, if you really want to know.

ARNIE. I'm not out of touch with you. I can see, for example, that you are embarrassed at being here, anxious to conceal it and looking forward to the moment when you leave and can tell the people outside how I am looking and behaving, and the things I say. As for Maureen—I can see how my behaviour has licensed what was previously impossible. Does that sound like someone out of touch with you?

HANSON. You take to insanity, Arnold, like other men take to drink.

(*Silence*)

ARNIE. You have insufficient innocence to be a fool, Jeffrey.

(*Silence*)

MAUREEN. We're still struggling along, by the way, Arnie, with rehearsals.

HANSON. Oh, yes. I'm afraid your absence, old man, has been severely felt. And, somewhat ineffectually, I must confess, I have been obliged to take your place. . . .

ARNIE. Robin Hood!

HANSON. Ah, yes!

ARNIE. Jeff, you must have discovered it for yourself.

HANSON. Yes?

ARNIE. A usurper. An outlaw!

HANSON. Ah, yes.

ARNIE. Always on the outside of things, Maureen—cynical of the established order: disenfranchised, dispossessed. A refugee, if you like, from the proper world.

MAUREEN. Yes.

ARNIE. That's how you should rehearse it.

HANSON. Yes.

ARNIE. I hope you've kept them to it, Jeff.

HANSON. Well, as a matter of fact . . .

ARNIE (*rising, with a dramatic self-gesture*) Kings!

JOAN (*to Arnie*) Why don't you sit down?

ARNIE (*moving down* R) They're a sort of receptacle, if you like. Into which flow all the goodness and intentions of mankind: and out of which in turn flow benevolence—and decisions. Authority. Rule. One becomes a king, not by chance—but by right: attributes fed in long before conception. Preordained.

HANSON. Well, we weren't making it that complicated. (*To Joan*) Robin stood on his bow yesterday afternoon and nearly guillotined his ear.

ARNIE (*moving* C) You think kingship's something foreign to me, Jeff? Let me tell you—I've studied it all my life. It's my profession. History—you think I come from an age sentimental about its motives. You're wrong. My ancestry is rooted in action, in events, not causes. It's only fools who worry why they are. (*He pauses*) Do you know what goodness is?

HANSON. Goodness? (*He glances at the others*)

ARNIE. Do you know what evil is? (*He looks round at them: they don't answer. He moves down* R *above the sofa, and to* C) Look. A simple arithmetical problem—set in all the schools. Take what we are from everything and what remains?

HANSON (*after a pause*) I don't know.

(ARNIE *looks at Maureen*)

MAUREEN. No.

ARNIE. Goodness and kings. (*He studies Hanson a moment*) Kings rise above themselves. They become—inanimate. Formed. (*He shapes it with his hands, then looks round at them*) Do you know what the greatest threat to the present century is? (*He pauses*) The pygmies. (*He smiles at them*)

HANSON. Yes.

JOAN. Arnie . . .

ARNIE. So small, so inconspicuous, they infiltrate everywhere. Not only out there, but into seats of government and power. And, of course, they're disguised. Not as men. Not even as small men. But as conditions of the soul. (*He relaxes*) You think that's a conspiracy? No. We *choose* the lesser men.

HANSON. Yes.

ARNIE. Napoleons—they have their day. Usupers, whether for good or ill. But the king rules not by revolution but by constitution. He is *born*: he is *bred*: is created king inside. (*He pauses*) His *constitution* makes *the* constitution which makes him king.

(JOAN *rises*)

(*Moving down* R) Joan, I don't like you standing behind me.

JOAN (*moving down* L) My mother's bringing in the tea. (*She holds open the kitchen door*)

(Mrs Ellis *enters with a laden tray and moves to the table to put it down.* Joan *follows*)

Hanson. Ah, good. Lovely.

(Mrs Ellis *nods without looking up*)

Arnie. Isn't that a miraculous sight? A tea-tray elevated through the air entirely by its own volition.

Joan. Arnie, I'm afraid, has taken to assuming my mother doesn't exist.

(Mrs Ellis *puts the tray on the table. She serves the tea according to instructions,* Joan *helping*)

Maureen. Milk and sugar?

Maureen. Thank you. We ought really to be leaving fairly soon. (*She looks at Hanson, and moves up to take her tea*)

Arnie. Oh, don't stay on my account, Maureen. I can perform miracles any time for your amusement. If you wish, I can make that tea-tray depart to where it came from entirely under its own resources.

Joan. Milk and sugar, Jeff?

Hanson. No sugar. I've decided I must slim.

Arnie. Or sugar transfer itself, unsolicited, from bowl to cup.

Maureen (*to Hanson*) Aye, now . . . (*She returns to her seat with her tea*)

Hanson. That's to say, someone has decided for me.

(Joan *hands Hanson his tea. Arnie has been overlooked*)

Arnie. What's that!

(Joan *sits* l *of the sofa with her tea*)

Hanson. Look, Arnold.

(Mrs Ellis *sits* r *of the table*)

Arnie. *What?*

Hanson. You don't have to play these games for *us*.

Arnie. Oh?

Hanson (*taking the bull by the horns*) We're your friends. Whatever you do, you're a friend, and we're concerned for you. (*Looking at Joan and Mrs Ellis*) Look, I don't wish to embarrass you, Joan. But you understand?

Joan. Yes . . .

Hanson. So there's no need for this eccentricity, Arnie.

Arnie (*sitting on the coffee-table*) What are you trying to do, Jeff?

Hanson. I'm trying . . .

Arnie. Hoping to *ingratiate* yourself with me?

Hanson. I hope there's no need for me to do that.

Arnie. You're being very foolish. Do you know *anything*?

Hanson. It seems not.

Arnie (*hugely, carried away*) Scars . . . (*He holds out the palms of his hands, looking at them*) They inhabit the skin. They grow there after a while like natural features. Deformities actually acquire that authority. (*He looks up bitterly at Hanson*) Did you know? (*He pauses*) Remove them—and you remove life itself. Well?

HANSON. I don't know what you're talking about actually, Arnold.

ARNIE. I'm talking about—alternatives.

HANSON. Alternatives. I see.

ARNIE. To kingship. (*He stares fixedly at Hanson. Then he smiles. A moment later he relaxes completely*) Oh, Jeff. (*He laughs*) You looked positively embarrassed. Didn't he? Pompous, if I didn't know him better.

MAUREEN. Well . . .

ARNIE. Ah, come on, now Jeff. Fair's fair.

> "A friend"
> You old prigster!
> I know a man with two left feet
> Who'd rather be dead than be seen in the street;
> Yet the fellow would hardly have seemed such a sight
> If he hadn't have had two more on his right.

(*He laughs, spreading out his hands*) I shall now tell you a dirty history.

HANSON. I honestly think, Arnie, we've had enough.

ARNIE. History has always had a certain fascination for me.

MAUREEN (*rising and moving L of Hanson*) Joan. I really think we should be going.

ARNIE. The raising of Lazarus as a permanent act of restitution. (*Rising*) Kings, queens, emperors. Saints! Inhabited by one's own domestic soul!

(*The others are silent*)

Everything has to be defined. Yet how can you define anything except by its limitations? Why!—my limitations are limitless!

MAUREEN (*putting her cup on the table and moving to the door up L*) I really think we ought to be going, Joan, you know. We can pop in again, later in the week—if that's convenient.

(JOAN *rises, puts her cup on the table and moves to the door*)

JOAN. Oh—yes, any time you like.

(MRS ELLIS *rises*)

HANSON (*rising*) Well . . . (*He replaces his cup on the table*)

(MRS ELLIS *piles the cups on the tray*)

ARNIE. Do you remember Scott? . . . Scott!

HANSON (*moving to L of Arnie*) Arnie. I'd like . . .

ARNIE (*direct to Hanson*) Certain things can't be destroyed, however much you try. Rifles rust, erode, and fall apart. They become mechanically defunct. But swords, while rusting, too, preserve down to their last grain an emblem of the truth. Instruments of honour, which the world is a feebler place without! Dignity. (*He draws himself up*) The past brought down to us in swords!

HANSON. Arnie, we have to be going.

ARNIE. Ah, yes.

HANSON (*to Joan, moving to the door*) If there's anything we can do, Joan . . . You will let us know?

JOAN. Yes. Thank you.

MAUREEN. 'Bye, Arnie.

HANSON. Good-bye, Arnold.

ARNIE (*cheerfully*) Good-bye. Good-bye. It's been very good of you to come.

MAUREEN. Good-bye, Mrs Ellis.

(MRS ELLIS *nods and exits down* L *with her tray.* ARNIE *nods cheerfully.* JOAN, HANSON *and* MAUREEN *go into the hall, and* JOAN *sees them out through the front door. As they exchange farewells,* ARNIE *moves to the sofa and sits.* JOAN *comes back into the room and moves behind the chair down* LC)

JOAN. Do you want some more tea?

ARNIE. What? I don't know.

JOAN. Soon there'll be nobody coming here at all.

ARNIE. No. No. That's quite true. I look behind me, Joan.

JOAN. What?

ARNIE. I live. I go along. I look behind. And I see—not achievements towering in my path.

JOAN. No . . .

ARNIE. Ruins. I can see—wonderful. (*A vision rises before his eyes*) If I raise you to the status of a queen, do you think you could be realistic?

(JOAN *exits to the kitchen.* ARNIE *sits alone, abstracted, still, the sword in his hand. After a few moments* JOAN *re-enters, leading* MRS ELLIS *by the hand*)

JOAN. Arnie? Is there anything else you want?

ARNIE (*after a pause*) What?

JOAN (*passing Mrs Ellis in front of her towards Arnie*) My mother has something to tell you.

ARNIE. What?

MRS ELLIS. Arnie—(*She looks concernedly at Joan, and then clenches her own hands*) I—we've—I'll be leaving tomorrow.

ARNIE. What? What? Who said that? Who!

MRS ELLIS. Arnie. I'll be going tomorrow. I've found a room.

ARNIE. I could have sworn . . .

MRS ELLIS. It's a small flat, really.

(ARNIE *looks up*)

The place I've found.

ARNIE. It's you! It's you!

MRS ELLIS. Joan helped me to find it. And . . .

ARNIE. Look. You are, or are you not, *positively speaking*?

Mrs Ellis. I—it's already furnished.

Arnie. Well—at least that's clear. It would have been alarming, Joan, at this late hour, to have discovered—of all things—that I suffered from hallucinations.

Mrs Ellis. I think it's the best for all of us.

Arnie. I'm sure. Yes. Yes. I'm sure. I'm sure. (*Suddenly*) We've had a good time, Edie.

Mrs Ellis. Yes.

Arnie (*tapping the side of his head*) I had something then on the tip of my tongue. No. No. It's gone. It's gone.

Mrs Ellis. It's not far away—that I can't pop in from time to time.

Arnie. No, no. I'm sure. We have, after all—what have we? What? This is extraordinary. After all these years.

Joan. Yes.

Arnie. I'd say . . .

Joan. Yes?

Arnie. That that was a revolution.

Joan. Yes.

Arnie (*rising*) Or a revelation. I'm not sure which. (*He pauses*) Ahem! (*He pauses*) I'd better make a speech. A moment like this— can scarcely go by. Unacknowledged.

Joan. I don't think it's necessary, Arnie.

Arnie (*moving* R) No? (*He puts down his sword on the coffee-table*) This is a very heavy sentence, Edie.

Mrs Ellis. I'm not sure . . .

Arnie (*moving* C) On us. On us. I might well have to make amendments. To the constitution. To accommodate that. (*He holds the top of his head*) It had been my intention—to leuchotomize my wife.

Mrs Ellis. Yes . . .

Arnie. Along with several others . . . As it is . . . (*He gazes up at them from beneath his hands*) We'd better have a party.

Mrs Ellis. After I've gone.

Arnie. Yes. Yes. After you've gone.

Mrs Ellis (*moving to the door up* L) I'll—go up. I've still some things to finish.

Arnie (*sitting on the sofa*) Yes. Yes.

(Mrs Ellis *exits to the hall and stairs. For a moment there is a silence*)

Back to school. Monday!

Joan. Yes.

Arnie. Rest. Recuperation. Work!

Joan. Yes.

(*There is a moment's silence.* Joan *moves* C)

Arnie (*suddenly, crying out*) Oh!

Joan. Arnie!

Arnie. Oh! There's something coming out!

Joan. Arnie . . .

ARNIE. Oh dear, Joan.

JOAN. Arnie—it's all right.

ARNIE. Oh dear, Joan. There's something here—that's very hard. Merciless. I can hear things. Breaking. I can hear things breaking up.

JOAN. Arnie—it's all right.

ARNIE (*rising*) Oh dear. Oh! (*He covers up his head*)

JOAN. Arnie.

ARNIE. Oh dear. Oh dear.
>   There's something. What?
>   Oh dear.
>   There's something coming out.

JOAN. Arnie.

(ARNIE *looks up, still holding his head*)

Come on, now.

ARNIE. Oh. Oh. (*His hands are clasped to the top of his head*) What am I to do?

JOAN. Here. (*She holds out her hand*)

ARNIE. Oh. *NOW!* (*He screams, hugely*)

(*There is a moment's silence*)

JOAN. It's all over.

ARNIE. Oh dear. (*After a moment he lowers one hand and after some hesitation takes hers*) Oh, I'm sure—I think.

JOAN. Yes.

ARNIE. In all sincerity. (*He calms. He looks slowly round*) Nevertheless, I'm assuming that I can come out. The assumption is merely based, you understand, on a generality of feeling.

JOAN. Yes.

ARNIE. Oh. Oh, lovely woman—feel no obligation;
>   Beauty is its own salvation:
>   The rest is meant to burn.

(JOAN *offers him her other hand*)

I can't hear a thing.

JOAN. Are you coming up?

ARNIE. Up?

JOAN. Yes.

ARNIE. Have I finished? (*He looks round*)

JOAN. Yes.

ARNIE. I've finished?

JOAN. I think so.

ARNIE. Are you sure?

JOAN. Yes.

ARNIE. Oh. Oh. Oh. Joan.
>   Oh. Joan.
>   Thank God.

The LIGHTS *fade to a Blackout, as—the* CURTAIN *falls*

FURNITURE AND PROPERTY LIST

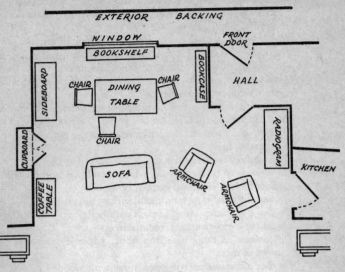

ACT I

SCENE I

On stage: Coffee-table (down R). *On it:* ashtray

Sideboard (up R). *On top:* tablecloth with knives and forks on top of it. *In drawer:* scissors

Bookcase (under window up C). *On top:* ashtray. *In shelves:* books

Bookcase (up LC). *On top:* ashtray. *In shelves:* books, odd articles

Radiogram (up L). *On it:* ashtray, bottle-opener

Dining-table (up RC)

3 chairs (R, L and below dining-table)

Sofa (RC). *On it:* cushions, paper, string

Armchair (C). *On it:* cushion

Armchair (down LC). *On it:* cushion

In cupboard R: broom, squeezy mop, umbrella

On wall above sideboard: loaded rifle

On floor C: suit of armour with detachable sword, paper, string, label

On hooks in hall: JOAN's coat

On wall below hall door: mirror

Carpet

Window curtains
Net curtains

NOTE: The following included ARNIE's "collection" as used in the London production:

On coffee-table: owl, bottle like bark, cylinder, conch shell, moss on stand. *On wall above:* poster, small piece of bark, cycle handle, metal disk

Over cupboard: tom-tom with rifle-butt hanging from it

On sideboard: Calor-gas top, clock, flue pipe, metal stand, toast rack, cruet, square concrete block, guttering, mats. *On wall above:* 2 tomahawks, flagon, shovel. *On shelf above:* paper cone, ship, wooden pot, leather belt

On floor up R: tree-trunk, large piece of asbestos, boomerang.

On wall up R: petrol tank, tin lid, poster, piece of bark

On shelf above window: 2 elephants, asbestos, cylinder, piece of concrete, brick

Over window: regimental mace

On bookcase up C: metal vase, whip, metal piping, pipe, broken cider flagon, electrical gadget, bowl, box

On wall L *of window:* 2 fans, metal spring, tin, poster

On floor L *of window:* long branch with bells hung on, lobster pot

On wall up L *above hall door:* metal stirrup

On bookcase up LC: press, iron hook, papier-maché urn, lock, piece of metal

On floor above bookcase: wooden stove with wooden golden vase and record-player turntable on top

On floor below bookcase: red drum with cheese on top and shell on top of cheese

On shelf above hall door: golden eagle and bundle of wood

On hall door: poster

On wall L *of door:* poster, small sieve

On floor L *of door:* rock

On radiogram: round sieve with Belisha beacon on top, record sleeves, rose vase, tin with pipe, round red tin

On corner of mirror: aeroplane

On wall below radiogram: poster, small wicker basket, grille

On kitchen door: poster

Off stage: Tray with 3 cups, 3 saucers, 3 spoons, butter dish, jam, milk-jug, small plate, breadboard with bread, sugar-bowl (JOAN)
Briefcase (ARNIE)
Teapot, poached egg on plate (MRS ELLIS)
Comic (ARNIE)

Personal: JOAN: watch
ARNIE: watch
       pipe
       tobacco in pouch
       matches

SCENE 2

Off stage: Pint bottle of beer, half full, screw top (JOAN)
Half-pint bottle, full, flip top (ARNIE)

ACT II

SCENE 1

Strike: ARNOLD's raincoat
MRS ELLIS's coat and apron
JOAN's coat and apron
Tray
Tablecloth
Bottles

Set: Armour R of door
Briefcase on table
Books and pictures on table
Glass on sideboard
2 dusters and polish in hall
Lock cupboard

Off stage: Tray with 2 cups, 2 saucers, 2 spoons, teapot, sugar-bowl, milk-jug (JOAN)
Duster (JOAN)
Shopping-basket (MRS ELLIS)

Personal: HANSON: walking-stick
                    watch

SCENE 2

Strike: Armour

Set: Curtains closed

Off stage: Bottle (MRS ELLIS)
Carrier bag with half-pint and quart bottles of light ale (SHEILA)
Bottle of whisky, bottles of light ale (HANSON)
Tray with 2 cups, 2 saucers, 2 spoons, teapot, sugar-bowl, milk-jug (JOAN)
Tray with 3 tumblers, 3 whisky glasses, bowl of crisps, bowl of peanuts (SHEILA)
Telegram (HANSON)

Personal: MRS ELLIS: handkerchief

ACT III

SCENE 1

Strike: All props and dressing *except:*
Ashtrays

Vase on radiogram
Record sleeves
Toast rack
Mats
Cruet
Clock
Books

Set: Armour in pieces on sacking between sofa and chair with eagle
and sword on top
Large box above kitchen door
Dustpan and brush between armchairs
3 empty bottles on coffee-table
Tray with 2 cups, 2 saucers, 2 spoons, milk-jug, sugar-bowl,
half-full coffee-pot, on table
Glass on sideboard
Curtains closed

Off stage: Suitcase (Mrs Ellis)
Glass of milk (Joan)

Scene 2

Strike: Armour
Tray from table
Suitcase
Box

Set: Repaired panel on cupboard
Vase of flowers on coffee-table
Vase of fruit and runner on sideboard
Vase of flowers and mat on table

Off stage: Wicker basket with shopping (Mrs Ellis)
Towel (Arnie)
Sword from armour (Arnie)
Parcel (Hanson)
Tray with 4 cups, 4 saucers, 4 spoons, teapot, milk-jug, sugar-
bowl (Mrs Ellis)

LIGHTING PLOT

Property fittings required: wall brackets

INTERIOR. A sitting-room. The same scene throughout

THE APPARENT SOURCES OF LIGHT are—by day, a window up C; by night, wall brackets

THE MAIN ACTING AREAS are—down R, up R, RC, C, up LC, down LC, up L

ACT I SCENE 1. Afternoon

To open: Effect of afternoon light

Cue 1   ARNIE exits   (Page 14)
            Fade to Blackout

SCENE 2. Evening

To open: Blackout

Cue 2   ARNIE switches on lights   (Page 14)
            Snap on wall brackets and interior lighting

ACT II SCENE 1. Afternoon

To open: As Act I Scene 1

Cue 3   JOAN: "Your coat"   (Page 33)
            Fade to Blackout

SCENE 2. Evening

To open: Blackout

Cue 4   At start of scene   (Page 33)
            Fade up to lighting as Cue 2

ACT III SCENE 1. Morning

To open: Curtains closed, room dim

Cue 5   JOAN draws curtains   (Page 54)
            Bring up lighting to full daylight

Cue 6   ARNIE: ". . . I should have done"   (Page 59)
            Fade to Blackout

SCENE 2. Evening

To open: Blackout

Cue 7   At start of scene   (Page 59)
            Bring up lighting as Cue 2

EFFECTS PLOT

ACT I

SCENE 1

No cues

SCENE 2

Cue 1   JOAN: ". . . you've gone to school"   (Page 17)
Dance music

Cue 2   ARNIE switches off radiogram   (Page 18)
Music off

ACT II

SCENE 1

No cues

SCENE 2

Cue 3   JOAN: ". . . I've had all day"   (Page 46)
Dance music

Cue 4   ARNIE switches off radiogram   (Page 47)
Music off

ACT III

SCENE 1

No cues

SCENE 2

No cues